~~CABAL~~ SKRPT
[1665-70s script]
A ~~S~~tories Prediction

David Gomadza

Tomorrow's World Order

A Stories Prediction

DEDICATION

A better world.

ACKNOWLEDGMENTS

Tomorrow's World Order

1 CHAPTER

A Stories Prediction: Swindling government money? Corrupt? Or just another bunch of just-us-only egoists. Or the way politics should be?

Tories and the Whigs were created in the 1660s so forever will look at this period with great admiration.

Outright: Any government that takes everyone back to the 1660s is not only bent but not fit for modern times in light of the human rights earned over the centuries. Surely you can't say life in the 1660s is the same as life in the 2020s. A country that relies on the tactics used in the 1660s will find a hidden modern secret digital equivalent of the methods and tactics used then to recreate the times of that age.
It is an undisputed fact that some countries view the 1660s as the best times where they simply gained economic advantage through easy trade in commodities including slaves.

Why would a modern 'civilised government' go back as far as the 1660s?
The element of prediction, a competitive advantage of knowing how the future will unfold simply because they are using a documented script but one only, they know about or one that very few people will know about.

Above all, only they among a few have documented every document and event going back as far as the 1600s thereby giving them a competitive advantage. I think the very argument they have used over years to provide solutions to all modern-day problems is simply comparing events of long ago and the modern ones and using the solutions then. A topic I will devote to later.

But we also know very well about the third-type error where a correct solution is prescribed to a wrong problem. Even if it is a great solution the fact that it is not a correct solution to the problem at hand will escalate the issues. Unless this is the intended way in which it becomes a malicious or deceptive act to gain unfavourably.

I know now this will sound out of context, but it will make sense later.

Straight to the point of the subject matter.

1. The Tories simply visit a time in the past e.g. centuries ago for solutions etc. This is reflected in their policies which are conservative in nature. Not that it is wrong, no. They have the right to be what they are and what they want. But we are saying that too much reliance on the past for everything will always create conflicts, misunderstandings, indirect abuses of power, etc. Simply because we are living in different periods. Picture people in the 1660s; what they want and how they perceive the world then. Now picture a modernised Britain full of foreigners with different attitudes altogether.

2. I know one would argue that there is nothing wrong with that and it is only a matter of finding the right balance between balancing the conservation of a people's culture and way of living and the integration of modern systems. But this applies only if it's about balancing the past and the future. But in the case of the Tories, I argue that it's more of going back to the 1660s and finding ways of accommodating the modern times into this 1660s mindset. It's not about balancing no but about modernizing the 1600s. Finding digital solutions that represent the 1600s and using this to recreate the 1600s. A perfect example is the use in humans of drone technology, digital hacking, and electromagnetic nerve tampering where in the name of

medical records everyone is chipped at birth and then goes on to be abused throughout life remotely. If they complain they are regarded as hallucinating simply because they thought it could not be proved. Then replace all traditional techniques of torture like hooding with a cloth with a digital form of hooding where the chip with rotary functions will twist the eye iris at an angle to the eye socket so that vision is lost even if the eyes are open as the eye iris is hidden inside the eye socket. Or white noises whereas with the traditional one's noises are used to confuse and stress a person to breaking points. Now they do the same using the chips to replay recordings in the person's ears deep inside and at a low volume that it is heard as inner voices. All this is made possible by a Blackbox so small that it is part of the chip. The recorded songs are then replayed to that person and only that person can hear this. In some cases, the recordings are replayed as a person is deep in sleep as in hypnosis in that the person when hearing these small voices the brain will convert these into pictures so that the person thinks he or she was dreaming. This is important in that this will also explain the rise of terrorists who if the inner small voices are played to them, might believe for real that it was a message from Allah. Ever wonder why terrorism is associated with very religious people? Could digital technology be the basis of all this or is there a real God or Allah commanding these people to go and kill others?

3. We also know for a fact that most foreigners born in this country are secretly hacked on birth without consent etc. simply because they are foreigners. The fact that they insist on hacking as a way of becoming British through the demands of the monarch and pledges to the monarchy. It can be argued that chances are that all foreigners born here are chipped. I don't care for whatever reasons. The Russia/Ukraine war has highlighted drone technology and its uses. Could the claims of the early 2000s be regarded as truthful that the West are implanting miniature versions of plane parts in humans namely; a miniature rotary propeller the size of the top index finger implanted at birth on the

lumbar bone; an electric diode fired into the left side of the lower body; a GPS chip; a miniature Blackbox or chip linked to the Blackbox to record and replay everything; a remotely operated link for the joystick they use to control this?

4. Another form of torture is the use of food and water to control the people. Traditionally it would involve the withdrawal of these physically, but the modern version would be to use all the parts mentioned above. The GPS tracks everywhere where the person has gone, everywhere the person gets help and every possible place of help and uses the chip to identify phone numbers around the radius of the position of the subject and phone all not to help that person in a digital scorched earth policy.

5. I mentioned that above so that you have a clear view of the issues to be discussed below. You can see outright that the technology exists and therefore what will be argued below is not hallucinations as they will try to convince you. But the reality is that the Tories are busy looking for advanced digital technologies that do the same acts as in the 1660s when they benefited from free labour and easy control of the people through force. But this is not the main topic of this document. Our concerns are with the trickery that this produces.

6. To prove that we are telling the truth we will predict what the Tories will do and how they arrive at such a decision. We will give you concrete examples of the past in the 1660s.

Our Tories Predictions.

1. Will swindle money from the government. Taxpayers' money by creating scandals and resigning at a cost to the taxpayers of around £230 000 [2x115000] per year for life. We believe the resignations have not stopped. Even the current prime minister might resign [19 November 2022] and be replaced by another Tory member. All this is at the expense of the taxpayers. Ok, governments make mistakes but what if they have created a loophole deliberately?

2. What matters even if they lose in the 2024 elections when four or five of them are still being paid a prime minister's salary or pension?

3. The insistence on being a member of the Church of England will see the prime minister secretly promise to change religion if he has to remain in power or this will be his reason to resign so that Torie's field another candidate to take the prime minister role all this at the expense to the taxpayers. That the current prime minister will be given a pension for life and the new prime minister and all those who resigned will also be entitled to the pension.

4. The current prime minister will try to introduce religious freedom at number 10 but this as I said might be the source of tension since he has a different religion.

5. By 2024 the Tories will have fielded 5 prime ministers most through resignations with a pension of around £230 000 – £575 000 per year for life.

6. The UK prime minister will offer to train 6000 Ukraine civilians as military personnel for a fee of £160 000 per year.

7. The prime minister will introduce a health fee of £10 of some sort [hearth tax].

8. The prime minister will favour the Russia and Ukraine war and religious freedom, and these will bring him into conflict with English members of parliament.

9. The prime minister will try to change some restrictive laws but will come into conflict with parliament. He will be challenged that the prime minister does not have powers to reverse laws passed by parliament.

10. The prime minister will encourage and support the war for England to gain a better trade position as its two major competitors in Russia and Ukraine will have been taken out of the picture. But over months and years will not benefit from this war.

11. The parliament will oppose the prime minister regarding him as interested in foreign affairs rather than the welfare of the British people who at some point will oppose any foreign aid as things become tough at home.

12. The prime minister might be bribed with a pension to resign and let an English person be put back as prime minister to keep things as they were.
13. The prime minister will focus more on health especially in the investigation of blood-related outbreaks, increasing testing centres, and showing interest in scientific pursuits.
14. The UK will now under this prime minister put more focus on the space race aiming to be the number one through funding of space projects.
15. Under this prime minister, the government will increase personal surveillance with more cameras making England a big brother nation where they observe people.
16. Absolute government. This government will try to abandon all international laws in favour of local laws.
17. People will refuse to pay taxes just as they will declare that as a family, they did the same.

Proof that the Tories are going back in time to the 1660s and recreating events to get a competitive advantage.

RECREATION OF THE 'CABAL' KNOWN AS THE SKRPT

Our arguments that the Tories are going back to the 1660s for answers is evidenced by their recreating of the CABAL during Charles II of England but one we gave the acronym of SKRPT based on the initials of the group. Moreover, this SKRPT went on to take important posts in the government. The main emphasis is that they went on to take top positions in the government. King Charles II had a privy council that is a private council to advise him. He had five members going by the acronym of CABAL. These people could run the country effectively and most were closely linked to the monarchy. So, in fact, they were there to represent the interest of the monarchy. To source funding for the monarchy through customs and excise duty and other innovative taxes like the Hearth Tax. This is because the income the King received from Parliament wasn't enough. At the time of 1665-1670, the King had an annual income of £1,2 million. This wasn't enough and worse the money was received way too late he had to go some time without these funds. This meant that he had to rely mainly on customs and excise duty funds. The cabal was a private group that enabled the King to ignore and dissolve the Parliament as these were capable of running the country.

This group worked as one powerhouse where power was equally shared among the five including the King. This meant all working together as one. All felt equally important and would all share responsibilities and tasks. In light of this information, you can see that they all would give each other a chance. That means if one fails then the other knowing that part of the group is equally important would step down for the other. That means each giving the other a chance. They all worked together for one goal and the King then even encouraged them to fight and quarrel as a way to deceive the people so as if they look like in-fighting only because they were to raise money for the king that could have attracted more scrutiny from the people. The CABAL's main task was to overhaul the King's finances. The King had chosen CABAL over the Parliament because the Parliament did not offer the King enough money to run the country. A budget of £1.2million was not enough for the king. So, this CABAL felt privileged to be chosen over Parliament as the king kept dissolving Parliament in favour of these. To keep in the king's favour, the CABAL had to do more for the king. Money was a big issue due to the First and Second Anglo War and the plague of 1665 and the Great Fire of London 1666. To be in favour of the king the CABAL had to be innovative and find new sources of income for the king. To supplement his income to run the country the king introduced a Hearth Tax among income from customs and duty.

SKRPT

The SKRPT is the modern version of the CABAL; young, ambitious, and energetic but just like the CABAL there to serve the Prime Minister [PM] in modern times. That is to find ways of generating money for the PM. The former PM appointed all the members of the SKRPT into government. If they are following the CABAL script it follows also that they are there to serve the interest of the PM who appointed them. Meaning that just like the CABAL there are there to look for money for the PM. The CABAL was a private group capable of running the country just as the PM.

Just like the CABAL, their utmost loyalty is to the PM, the one who appointed them. Even though they might have conspired to force the PM to resign, their interest is for the PM. We believe that all this was a calculated plan.

1. The PM faces a financial crisis with inflation and Britain at risk of a recession. We believe that the plan was for the PM to temporarily step back and resign through a scandal. Since power is shared between the PM and the five members of the SKRPT. If the PM steps down any member of the SKRPT would step in his shoes and create means for fundraising for the PM knowing that he would return and take over. This means implementing controversial policies.

a]
Financial Exigency. This means the need for drastic means to deal with the dire financial situation. This triggers the need to levy taxes.

The Clever bit. [Just an opinion]
The idea from the word go is to increase taxes to close the deficit gap through taxes. But increasing taxes makes a PM very unpopular. So, credibility and trust of the PM are very critical here. The PM might have promised that he would not increase taxes, but he needs to plug the gap between income and expenditure and this can only be done through increased taxes. So, the PM recruits the SKRPT. Ever heard of those managers to save their face who hire a friend to sack the friend and gain an advantageous position? But the plan here is to offer 'imaginary tax cuts' first to raise the hope of the people in a psychological manner in which corporations and wealthy individuals will welcome the tax cuts with open arms. But the PM can't offer tax cuts because everyone knows that he is in a financial black hole. So, through a scandal, he resigns after secretly negotiating with one of the SKRPT for the SKRPT to come in and do his dirty work but quits too after the dirty work has been done. The view is that when one of the SKRPT
resigns people would put the PM back who then goes on to increase taxes even higher than they were before the mistake of the SKRPT.

King Charles II entered into a secret treaty with king Louis XIV where he was promised a pension of £230 000. If the PM would help one of the SKRPT both would earn a pension of £230 000. [2x115 000].
The current pension for a PM is only £115 000 and to be able to follow the 1665-1670 script, resigning from office would make sure that the pension to the PM and one of the SKRPTs would be double that to £230 000.
b] Trickle-down economics.

Trickle-Down Economics.

These are economic policies that are adopted and implemented that offer huge tax subsidies to the highest earners, the upper-income class, huge corporations, and wealthy individuals in the hope that this increases growth and then the benefits gained by these upper-income groups will be trickled down to the poor people. In this case, governments offer huge tax cuts to the top brass hoping that these in turn will offer benefits also to those at the lower levels.
The method advocates for tax cuts or lower taxes for corporations and rich individuals who in turn would create more jobs etc and all this is believed to benefit the lower-class people.
a] The abolishing of the 45% higher tax income.
b] Lifting of the stamp duty threshold.
We can only infer that it was to offer the biggest tax cuts to the rich and corporations by abolishing the higher rate of income tax paid by everyone earning above £150 000 a year. The government will then have to borrow large sums at ever-increasing expensive rates hoping to use government powers in the future to stop the exchequer. Meaning using government powers to stop repayments for twelve months citing reasons like say the funding of the Russia/Ukraine war or a higher budget deficit. Hoping that in the end all this would simply be regarded as the economic national debt that will be paid off in years to come. Resign to let a bad but critical decision be taken by your successor and then return after the decision has already been taken and the successor had resigned then correct and go further than resign status.
Once back in power then actually increase taxes even higher than they were before.

Even though in this situation the PM did not return to take his initial PM position, the next PM who took over now drastically implemented policies to correct the mistake by actually increasing even higher taxes. This way the corporations and higher earners would not complain that they would feel like the government was willing to offer them a tax cut so they would not mind paying even more taxes in return.

SOURCES
OF REVENUE CUSTOMS AND DUTIES [literally] as in customs of the conservatives or customary to the conservatives for corporations and high earners to donate funds to the Tories as their duty.

I mentioned above that the King's allowance of £1,2m wasn't even so he needed other sources of income. Above all, there were not enough ways the King would collect or get this money from the parliament. So he emphasised the collection of customs and excise duty.
The duty which is levied on the goods which are manufactured in the country is called excise duty whereas the duty which is levied on the goods which are imported from a foreign country is called custom duty.
Wikipedia.

The 45% tax cut will increase the custom and excise duties in that a lower tax rate for corporations will trigger growth as production will increase. This will also mean increased imports. This can also point to the fact that collecting taxes might not be effective in solving the government's finances. This is because there is too much competition for taxes and national insurance collected. In the form of the police and the NHS who are funded as well by these funds.

The Deception. [Still an opinion.]

1. But we believe that this is more than what the Tories want you to believe.

The trickle-down policy in the 45% tax cut for corporations will only benefit the Tories rather than the government. This is because the 45% tax cut will put extra income in the pockets of wealthy people and corporations. The very people who can donate to the Tories rather than alleviate economic inequalities? It is absurd to think that giving corporations extra money in tax relief will see the poor or middle class benefiting from this. If the government wants to reduce inequality it will cut tax rates for this group. No evidence that offering corporations and wealthy citizens tax reductions will result in reduced poverty among the people.
We believe all this is to bribe corporations and wealthy individuals in a scratch my back and I will scratch yours act where the Tories will say we reduce taxes for you so donate to our party.

1.   We also believe that the tax cuts are meant to make corporations, banks, and wealthy individuals feel free and easy to lend and to offer loans to the Tories. We also believe that at some point the Tories might default to repay these loans. Or defer payment making some of these corporations bankrupt etc. Just an opinion.

THE GOLDSMITH BANKERS AND THE STOP OF THE EXCHEQUER

King Charles II faced financial problems namely, a lack of funds and the need to fund the Third Anglo-Dutch war so he delayed debt repayment for 12 months this made some goldsmith bankers go bankrupt.

HOW ARE THE TORIES FUNDED? COLLECTION OF DONATIONS AS A TRICKLE-DOWN EFFECT.

Could the tax cut to corporations and the wealth be a bribe and incentive for them to donate to the Tories in the future? Or just a means to increase production and imports to increase the custom and excise duty?
So, could the Tories be using 1665 onwards Charles II and CABAL [SKRPT] I mean script?

Having said all this it follows also that the Tories are aware of what they are doing. They are simply going to the past for answers. Even if they argue that they are or were not aware of the CABAL and the reign of Charles II they are in a position of trust and must act in the public interest.

One can argue that they might be creating scandals as a means to an end. A way of fulfilling their goals of draining the government coffers as they resign and letting some of theirs have a piece of the cake as well. Can ignorance be relied upon?

If unaware of Charles II's partying that earned him the title of the Merry Monarch then the past PM's partying that earned him the title associated with Partygate could be just a coincidence.

Maybe we need to wait to see how it goes first with the new PM and see how he fits into this 1665 onwards SKRPT [script].

But so far, he is going according to the script. We have seen his emphasis on the £10 health levy synonymous with Charles II's hearth tax.

Could the new PM just like Charles II later promise to convert from his religion Hinduism to the Church of England or he will push for a Declaration of Indulgence that favour religious freedom?

We also believe that he might be offered or is automatically entitled to a pension even if he resigns as well. Or someone will make a deal or secret treaty to offer him money so that he resigns to keep English-speaking members on the throne as before.

Russia/Ukraine War vis a vis Second Anglo-Dutch War.

It seems the new PM has already jumped into the last PM's shoes of supporting the war. We all know that Britain won't benefit much from this war. Would he play a bigger part in peace talks or will do whatever it takes to prolong the war hoping to disrupt Russia and Ukraine's whole trading position? Or just like every country, he is about offloading unwanted weapons to increase the manufacturing of new ones to fight inflation and boost the economy. All this is at the expense of Ukraine women and children who are dying every day.

We would like to think that Scotland is in the same shoes as the Ukrainians. If so, would that be hypocrisy to fight for Ukraine whilst oppressing Scotland?

Are you sure all this is about Ukraine's sovereignty?

Or just like Charles II, Britain triggered the war by making Ukraine fight a proxy war? All this is to gain a competitive advantage in world trade. To put Russia and Ukraine out of global trade for more than a good 2 years. It can be argued that Britain has a direct link to Ukraine. They are training the Ukraine's for a fee of £160 000 each year Just like Charles II who made a treaty with Louis XIV. In return, Louis had to supply 6000 troops to Charles II. As with the PM, he will train 6000 Ukrainian troops in the UK.

Check out how accurate our Russia and Ukraine war prediction are in a book titled A Perfect Russia-Ukraine War/Military Operation prediction.
https://play.google.com/store/books/details/David_Gomadza_A_Pe
rfect_Prediction_Russia_Ukraine?id=PmaVEAAAQBAJ&gl=GB

If our prediction is super correct, then the war is to last in 2024 July unless we intervene or someone else intervenes.

Could the UK keep escalating the war just to drive their economy and alleviate global problems?

There are so many points that you can easily tell that the Tories if not using 1665-onwards script to run the country. Then they might have created their SKPRT but one so similar to the Charles II era even if they try to change some aspects here and there.

If they are innocent, then it could be the third party. The 'Wagner' group is in the form of the NHS. Who pretends to advise where they have illegally chipped and hacked everyone since birth and all they do now is snoop and put big brother surveillance on all your activities and ill advise so that you make those you work for losing money. Money that they will end up gaining as they will tell you that they have orphans to feed. If they don't trick you to lose money how will they end up feeding the orphans they have raised through the NHS teaching hospital?

If you are new to Britain, you might think that they are working hard and doing a great job until you discover how the orphans end up orphans.

It was them who stole their parents from them. It was they who tortured [through chipping at birth- electromagnetic nerve tampering – drone technology in humans] the orphan's father to breaking points and offered their heroin from their fields that caused the death of this poor orphan's father. All this grooming the orphan as a child soldier to fight foreigners.

Then you will realise that this country for real is still in the 1660s. They are using Christopher Wren manuals on colony collapse strategy.

To them, the 1660s is when the Tories were founded. The 1660s is when things were easy. They had a monarchy and all these human rights are just another pain in the butt for them. They want what worked for them. A world they control everyone. A world they would simply use the general's daughter. Time someone complain they would simply shout.

"Take him to the tower and give him the general's daughter."
On hearing this you would think it's a real person until you discover that the general daughter is a torturing device. Nowadays in the name of uniformity and the monarch just before you are granted British citizenship, they insist you have references who are English and who will guide you. These will tip you that you must be clean as the monarchy has to perform the citizen ceremony. Since you are from a continent not so trusted you must be checked first to make sure you are in good condition. Until you woke up feeling drugged and disoriented. You realise you are with people in a position of trust. They tell you everything will be okay. Six months later after all legal avenues to appeal if wronged by a doctor or hospital have elapsed. Then you realise that the general's daughter was a miniature rotary propeller into your lumbar bone. A remotely operated electric diode. All these use drone technologies and electromagnetic nerve tampering. Then you find out being abused remotely. You start reading that during Charles II foreigners who did not confirm were drawn {drone]
and waiting to be beheaded. In most circumstances, all you did is complain that this system is rotten. They are acting like we have no rights at all. They have stripped us of our hard-earned freedoms.

But they have done that. Imagine blacks in the 1660s. If everything they are doing is based in the 1660s then it follows too that there is no respect for other races in Britain. Even though they have a black person as part of the SKRPT and some in parliament. They all have been drawn [droned- implanted at birth with a rotary propeller and a needle diode to finish them off.] No respect for other races. Everything is institutionalised.
We devised an easy way to check. Follow these easy steps and find out for yourself.
Stand upright then look at your tailbone which is at the back move your head and eyes from left to right checking your left and right lumbar bones. See diagram below.

Having pointed to the CABAL and the SKRPT can it be inferred that someone might speculate that the Tories have devised a clever way to stay in power and to milk the system. Mind you all members of the CABAL or SKRPT have equal powers as power is distributed among all. Instead of being centred in the PM alone. So, they can easily resign to give their mates a chance at the PM post knowing that all Tories will be taking a huge lot from the government coffers. Yet they make policies to benefit the richest. Unless the money is expected to trickle down to their own Tories coffers. In that case they could be swindling money from the government. Or are they?
I have created so many situations that will trigger discussions about the Tories in power.

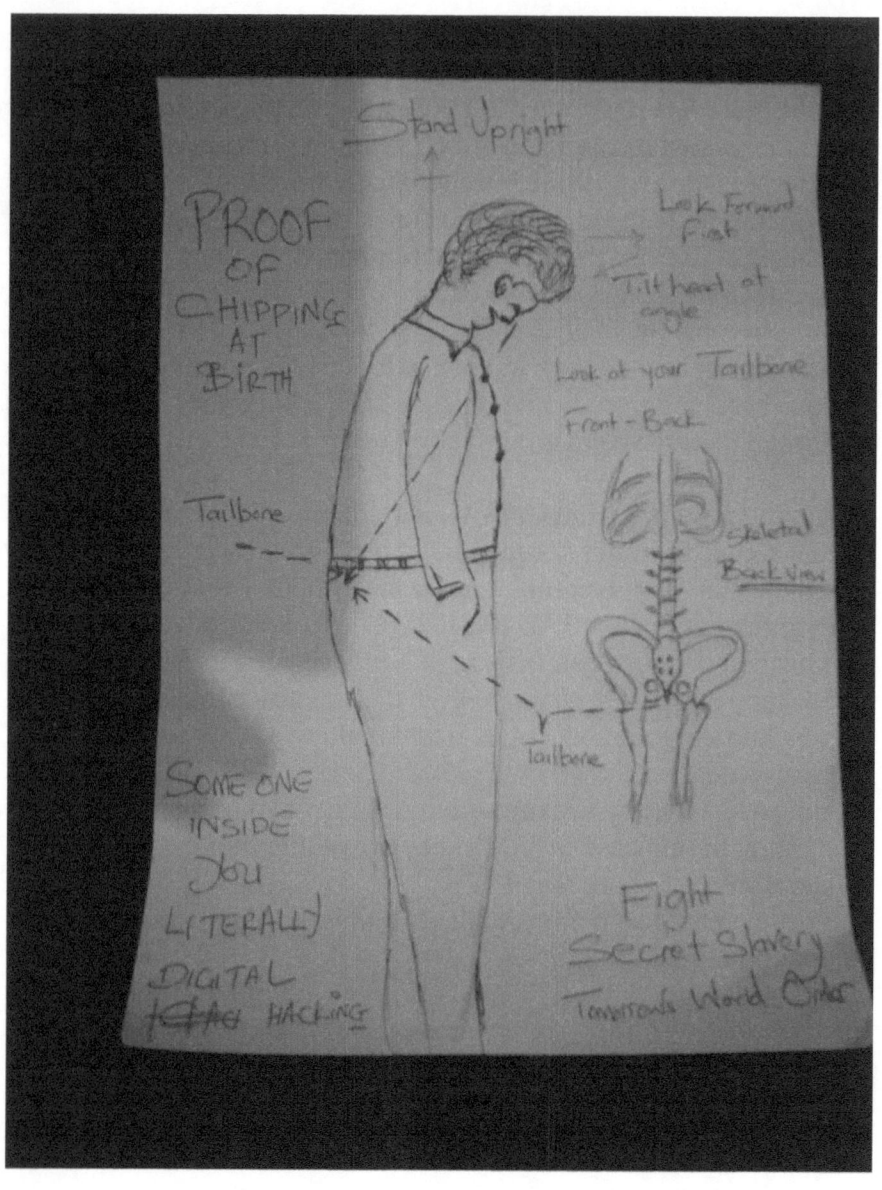

2 CHAPTER

TOMORROW'S WORLD ORDER THE ANSWER TO YOUR: -Our ability to hold Gov to account is under threat
TOMORROW'S WORLD ORDER
<tomorrowsworldorder@outlook.com>
2020-11-18, Tr 04:10
Kam:

Priedų: 2 (13 MB)
the one David Gomadza Tomorrow's world order (2).pdf; Evil Human hacking (1).

The British are trying to recreate KING JAMES II of London1665 onwards' life. The current PM technically and indirectly becoming one leader of Scotland and England. More and more he will try to dictate life for the Scottish as well hiding behind corona Covid virus pandemic until Scotland has no say in their country's politics. Loss of independence. Are you ready for indirect recolonisation?? They are going to break all international laws known to a man believing that only the government has the final say. But is that so? Put things in place now.

TOMORROW'S WORLD ORDER
<tomorrowsworldorder@outlook.com>

Išsiųsta: 2020 m. lapkričio 15 d., sekmadienis 09:20
Iki: comms@liberty-human-rights.org.uk <comms@liberty-human-rights.org.uk>; nadiaom@libertyhumanrights.org.uk <nadiaom@libertyhumanrights.org.uk>; sct@amnesty.org.uk <sct@amnesty.org.uk>; information@libertyhumanrights.org.uk <information@libertyhumanrights.org.uk> **Tema:** TOMORROW'S WORLD ORDER THE ANSWER TO YOUR: -Our ability to hold Gov to account is under threat

THIS IS NOT A CIRCULAR LETTER BUT AN HIGHLY IMPORTANT EMAIL. A MUST-READ.

Dear Your Honours, Sirs, and Madams.
 First and foremost, everything that is happening now is not by chance but a carefully written script - of past events going back as far as 1665 in Britain.
YOU MUST UNDERSTAND THAT THE CURRENT SYSTEM IS DESIGNED TO BE PREDICTABLE SO IT BENEFIT THOSE WHO HELPED PUT IT IN PLACE; namely the British. FACT. But before I go into the details you must understand who we are and how we will become YOUR BEST ANSWER to all government's created problems through their stubbornness etc.
 1.
Your Honour, ladies, and gentlemen we are a registered political party registered in Great Britain reg number 2331788. Registered by the Electoral Commission.
Check here
first. http://search.electoralcommission.org.uk/English/Registrations/PP10355? fbclid=IwAR3jj2YjEBCHaj3S6lNQV9i5pZcb9J8tLu3 cubiQanXpPRIKRjETpQF1L9c
Read this carefully.
I David Gomadza founded Tomorrow's World Order based on the notion I call God's Dilemma. A fundamental principle that proposes to counteract the ABSOLUTE POWER beliefs of current governments globally and the secret idea of the DIVINE RIGHT OF THE GOVERNMENT. I believe that our sole purpose on earth is to follow God's example of ruling the world as a unified whole as the ONLY SOLUTION to all global problems. Hence the rise of

Tomorrow's World Order. READ VERY CAREFULLY. I am not saying that I am God. No. But I am saying that we humans spend $trillions trying to create a robot that Acts, Thinks, and Behaves like a human. It is also true that God created us as humans to see if one of us can rise to the challenge and Act, Think, and behave like God too.

2. Whatever is happening today in the world, believe it or not, is going by the script with the NHS, doctors, the police, the monarchies, etc. being the directors. Believe me, the truth will shock you that these people are RECREATING PAST EVENTS, so they determine the future and have a competitive advantage at the expense of other people and HARD-EARNED FREEDOMS. This year 2019-2020 we are following the 1665 -1666 documented script. FACT.
Believe me the British are running the world, especially their government through the 1665-1666 history script.
Issues at the time.
i. The Black Death plague pandemic
ii. Britain was on its knees without money putting money in the war chest.
iii. Government/Monarchy's ABSOLUTE POWER
iv. Government/ Monarchy's belief in DIVINE RIGHT OF THE GOVERNMENT/MONARCHY etc.

3. The players or cast.
James II and his brother King Charles II played by PM.... Ladies and gentlemen, I present the cast and those who are RELIVING THEIR LIVES. THIS IS THE CRITICAL PART YOU MUST UNDERSTAND WHY WHATEVER IS HAPPENING IS HAPPENING. IT IS NOT A COINCIDENCE BUT A CAREFULLY CALCULATED SCRIPT AND PLAN.
 All said in bona fide and with due respect but you must understand the truth. PANDEMIC.
The NHS is like a film director. Ever been to the horses? Watching the horses running with the ambulance running on the road beside them with the sirens etc. controlling their start, their speed, and who is going to win using electromagnetic nerve stimulation and tampering acting like dog collars?

The current pandemic is not a coincidence. Whoever is behind it is using digital pathogens or newly engineered biologicals to imitate the black death plague of 1665-1666. Seen the literary killings of blacks from 2019 to 2020 in the USA mainly. I will explain why. GOVERNMENT'S ABSOLUTE POWER.

When King James II was in power, he believed in the king's Absolute power. No one had the power to challenge the government. They could simply override all international laws. He believed that no written laws would detect what the government does. This is what is happening now. THIS IS CRITICAL AND ADDRESSES THE PROBLEMS YOU ARE FACING AND GOING TO FACE BECAUSE IT IS GOING TO BE WORSE. FACT!!!!!

DIVINE RIGHT OF THE GOVERNMENT

James II believed that no one on earth can question the government, only GOD can. He believed that he was chosen even before he was appointed to office by God so whatever is happening is already written and must be done. This is exactly what the PM is supposed to believe too. The only difference here is that then it was not GOD but the NHS who did everything to RECREATE 1665 onwards London.

This is your challenge today as no one will have the power to challenge him legally. Honestly, this is happening now for I have studied the British and their use of secret TORTURE using advanced gadgets is the trigger to the rise of Tomorrow's World Order one in the footsteps of GOD the only power to stop change and amend the belief in ABSOLUTE POWER and the DIVINE RIGHT for the government now will be forced to acknowledge that it is not itself or the NHS guiding it and one with power to control it or challenge it but ONLY US as we stand for the DIVINE RIGHT in this contest. See attached book Tomorrow's World Order.

3 CHAPTER

TECHNICALLY THE GOVERNMENT IS ONLY
ANSWERABLE TO US TOMORROW'S WORLD ORDER.
We are a global political party. We aren't answerable to anyone.
We have rights to establish our courts that are adhered to by all.
We enforce all our laws through assassins when we are fully
active. We have the right to print and mint our own money
(currency). We will have our digital currency when fully
operational.

So, we are the solution to all global issues.
The current government will hide behind Covid 19 and fully
implement the Absolute Power and Divine Rights notions.
Breaking all international laws gives it so much power that it will
stampede all our hard-earned freedoms. This is because they are
using a Script that says that," a government is not accountable to
an earthly authority such as you or other rights organisations. This
is because their right to rule is derived from divine authority. That
is where we come in. The good thing is we are registered and have
developed a robust system of laws and enforcement to close all
loopholes they might take, and we can bring it to court for all the
crimes documented. BRITISH'S EXERCISING OF THEIR
ABSOLUTE POWER AND DIVINE RIGHT.
Chagos Case. The global community has advised or ordered them
to return the stolen land but since no authority on earth is qualified
to tell them what to do, they have defied all that. If push comes to
shove, we can prove that there are reasonable arguments that they
are exercising these beliefs, therefore, thinking they are above the
law. But no one is above the law.
We have reasons to believe that.
1. They might have triggered the 9/11 attacks to protect and install
fear in people to stop them from going back. Not to go back and
resettle at Chagos after the eviction.

2. Also giving the USA a good reason to justify occupying stolen islands to provide a war front to fight Iran and Iraq just in front of the Chagos.

3. Bringing back the USA into colonization despite the 1776 independence. Britain leased Chagos for a long lease to hold the USA for ransom. Once they have occupied stolen land, giving it up under pressure from human rights organisations will still make them liable to fulfil the lease agreement or be held in breach of the lease agreement thereby remaining in debt to Britain forever.

4. Britain can say it even LEASED America to the USA on a long-term lease just like they did with CHAGOS meaning indirectly still under British control bringing the 1776 independence into question.

5. The worst part is that the British will BLACKMAIL the USA in that using stolen land weakens their position as global leaders ending up doing what Britain wants.

a. OUR GREATEST FEAR AND SUSPICION is that they are secretly recreating the scenes just before the HIROSHIMA AND NAGASAKI ATOMIC BOMB. Right now, we believe the reason they refused to buckle to pressure is that they are planning a nuclear attack making nuclear weapons at Chagos. The reasons why they evicted everyone. To use after the Covid-19 pandemic as part of the SCORCHED EARTH POLICY to blister and wipe out the disease just like in Hiroshima and Nagasaki when their sanctions brought Japan to its knees just like in the holocaust with diseases etc. I argued in my book.

Tomorrow's World Order: A New Law & Order. Dealing with Threats of Invasions, Wars, and War Crimes
https://www.amazon.com/Tomorrows-World-Order-Dealing- Invasions/dp/B084DGX6QL/ref=mp_s_a_1_13? dchild=1&keywords=david+gomadza&qid=1605414036&sr=8-13

That they used TIME CAMPS instead of concentration camps but with the same desired effect through sanctions to cause diseases then use a nuclear bomb to clear and scorch the earth justifying that as the only solution to eradicate the disease.

AGAIN, YOU ALL MUST UNDERSTAND that after the 1665 black death pandemic there was a great fire of London in 1666.

A fire that we believe was triggered deliberately as a solution to the black death pandemic. It can't be a coincidence that this year there is Covid and the secrecy and refusal to give back Chagos can only mean that for years they have been preparing for the great atomic fire to end Covid one we believe is a man-made pathogen made in the lab or a digital one operated through human hacking and digital pathogens that imitate all Covid symptoms. Remotely operated using plane parts and satellite systems with GPS, recording properties, etc. to target and kill mainly developed-foreigners through a colony collapse strategy proposed by CHRISTOPHER WREN A BRITISH SCIENTIST IN 1654. The one whose ideas triggered the concentration camps; the Guantanamo bay cages and all today's Covid related glass quarantining camps. The man who is thought to have started documented blood transfusion and injection of substances into the bloodstream. We fear that they are planning Global human hacking and mass killing. We believe the Covid pandemic is used to test people. But during testing, the government is going to secretly implant advanced miniature plane parts, advanced small personal computers the size of a rice grain, and electrodes. Then electromagnetic nerve tampering triggers the Covid symptoms digitally and remotely. To kill people. So, the testing is a way to hack people or book them for future hacking then abuse them later mainly 6 months after their rights to appeal have expired to challenge them in courts. We have a video to prove that this happened before. See the evil hacking video attached.
6.
It could be China behind the Covid, but Britain might be taking advantage of the situation. If you look at the above 1665-1666 Black death and the great fire that followed. You will see that the reason for holding Chagos is for nuclear or other dangerous weapon manufacturing.

Our basis.
i. They did this before. Documented precedent that they can use a bazooka to kill a fly. Proof of Hiroshima and Nagasaki Atomic bombs. Therefore, irresponsible, and reckless.
ii. The issues of Covid to them will justify using nuclear weapons regardless. To scorch out the pandemic once and for all.

Something we can't tolerate as the new global leaders.

iii. Britain has no money or soon is going to face financial woes just like other countries with the NHS and the police Milking the system to breaking points causing the government to enforce lockdown to reduce the amounts of those doing overtime rather than controlling the pandemic.

iv. The fact that Britain just got out of Europe means they would rather leave or not react faster so that the Covid pandemic does maximum damage to clean the country. Again, the leaders were happy after the 1666-6 pandemic and great fire. Reduced government bills. The current burden is the pension bill- many old people- whom they regard as 'deadwood'.

v. The rise in abuse of other races evidenced by racism riots and demonstrations of 2020 we believe are just tests of how the people would react if they go on with their great atomic fire plan. A mass killing test drill.

vi. There are no courts equipped to deal with most issues like Chagos officially leaving all current courts only in advisory positions. Hence the rise of Tomorrow's World Order. But this is a loophole they can take and do harm by obliterating others using nuclear weapons and getting away with it.

vii. I argued in my book Tomorrow's World Order Dealing with threats of invasions that the fact that they got away with the HIROSHIMA AND NAGASAKI atomic use there is nothing to stop them from doing it again. The fact that they leased the Chagos to the USA is a cause of concern in that they will make the US fail to react as global leaders but go with the flow. True in the Iraq war during PM Tony Blair where they cooked/ falsified dossiers just to justify the 2003 war. Ever heard of an accomplice to a crime? The USA now can't condemn RECOLONISATION by Britain as they will simply say look who's talking. Britain can years later declare that it leased America to the USA just like they did with Chagos.

viii. The pact knows that no one in the world will stop them even the UN which declares that it can stop wars is useless in stopping wars. All are advisory useless institutions that act AS RUGBY PLAYERS who distract opposition so that their strikers the UK and USA score perfect tries/goals by giving everyone a false sense of security that they can stop wars when they can't.

The intended effects are that they will make those who might have reacted NOT react as they all will have assumed that the UN and others will stop wars until the minute they watch thousands of people scorched to death with an atomic bomb. Secondly, their presence puts everyone in a guilty position so that they can't react afterwards. This is because the people soon after will feel guilty for trusting the UN etc. to stop the war. They will also feel guilty for failing to anticipate that the UN is just a distractor and a psychological mind-playing body to let these barbarians kill women and children in cold blood as collateral.

ix. Lack of courts to deal with them.

All courts will mention that they have no jurisdiction to judge these, quoting rule 47. They have a systematic system that labels everyone who cries racism as mentally ill to cover the systematic racism. FACT. Then go on to abuse that person deliberately racially through hacking see the video attached labelled evil human-hacking. So, the person says it is abuse, so they are justified in telling everyone that he or she is mentally ill. So, they hack all foreigners and then use the plane parts; the rotary propellers, black boxes, GPS, and remote electromagnetic nerve tampering to damage that person's brain. A case of mass genocide killing blacks and destroying a race.

x. Linked to the above is the fact that they are using the mentioned plane parts and radiation to steal years off people's lives by greying their hair as a way of identifying them as mentally ill. As I said they deliberately racially abuse all blacks, so they cry racism and then label all as mentally ill over time. JUST watch the 2020 race demonstrations. Even though it was mainly in the USA they have a Mirroring method or twin countries or sister cities that whatever happens in one happens exactly in the other as well. This James II is the one The Duke of York; New York city had named after him.

xi. They know no one will believe that human hacking and control are happening. First, a hacker is also a torturer and a hostage taker, and a slavery master because the purpose is to hack and change then kill otherwise perfect systems. To us, this crime carries 3 life sentences or instant death to be shot in public by the approved assassins. There are slavery implications as well as a hacked person being a hostage and a slave. Speaking of recolonisation.

xiv. So, it is evident that the system is designed to act as it is doing to let those who helped create it remain to abuse people and use extreme force e.g. Hiroshima atomic as a show of power. We are against this. I wrote in my book Tomorrow's World Order Dealing with threats of invasions that to us the USA and UK have no license to plan, make, stockpile, use or distribute nuclear bombs after having recklessly used these in Hiroshima and Nagasaki. They automatically lost the right to a nuclear arsenal. If it wasn't for NATO, their leaders would have been dragged to court. But that is not to say they are getting away with murder under our system. No. We are introducing EMPATHY LAWS that we will use even to drag NATO leaders to court. No one is above our laws once we are fully functional.

xv. We will give the USA a chance to redeem itself from this RECOLONISATION or enslavement trap by offering them an opportunity to fulfil WAR PLAN RED. A chance to fight Britain for who they are a dark colonial slave master who has benefited from acts like slavery and still secretly doing the same. A plan to deal with Britain not just as a manipulating devious country but as a dark colonial power still doing the same; stealing and recolonizing countries using dirty tactics. Look at Chagos. Look at secret slavery. I was born in June 1976 when the Hooded Men case was brought to the high court against Britain on TORTURE and in 2020 I am a victim of torture by this regime as we speak and THEY ARE STILL DOING THE SAME 44 years later nevertheless hidden using secret plane parts and remote secret drone technology. A chance to redeem themselves from the Hiroshima and Nagasaki atrocities too as they were manipulated through faked dossiers as in the Iraq war of 2003 by Tony Blair. A chance to see that 9/11 was an emotional trauma that triggered attacks on foreigners when the likely suspects are the British. Read Chagos case law and see why they benefited from 9/11 or read the book I wrote. Carolinadeivid **The Vice President of Electronic transfer.**

See Chagos map and the 9/11 planes route on Wikipedia that looks like the twisted ankle map a resemblance to Chagos.

xvi. What they are doing is abolishing evil practices like slavery and hacking BUT going underground to DO EXACTLY THE ACT THEY HAVE JUST ABOLISHED. FACT!!!

xvii. They used slavery tactics to ship out people from Chagos carrying out a few in boats and ships and offloading them somewhere so that they are not detected or seen by the antislavery patrolling ships. The tactics used by banks to steal money from people through the PPI scandal

In a case, I fought Barclays the very person behind the PPI scandal refunds when I highlighted that they used tactics Britain used during slavery to transport slaves even after the abolishing. See links between the UK government and Barclays before the Payment Protection Insurance. I have emails to prove this.

xviii. I wrote a book on how to deal with countries like Britain who go on to cause problems globally creating and initiating what I called FOREIGN FRIGHTS funding terrorist activities abroad; stealing and planting landmines abroad so people end up coming to their countries; colonizing countries; making manmade viruses to use abroad to kill others so they end up coming to their countries; bombing countries with atomic weapons so the people's countries are toxic forever so that people end up coming to their countries; starting wars abroad to get expensive resources like oils. INDIRECT SLAVERY PEOPLE WERE FORCED TO COME ON THEIR OWN. Did you know that Britain made a statement that they were now able to repay the USA its World War 2 debt the day after Saddam Hussein was hanged? Offering old-dated Protection that turns people into terrorists or makes them carry out revenge attacks. Selling ideas, they tried and tested and went back in the past to recreate scenarios like the one today. 1665-1666 black death. 1295 by Edward 1's Edict of Eviction of the Jews a manual used by Hitler to give the Jews the final solution. Holocaust. Using scorched-out policies to impose sanctions that kill women and children.

4 CHAPTER

Solutions
Isolation
Sanctions

Lobby NATO to abandon Article 5 license to commit crimes regardless and make it be given on merit.

Drag the leaders to court on all crimes from the beginning of time WHENEVER IT CAN BE PROVED THAT they are still doing the same thing only now secretly hidden using advanced technology. Drag most useless institutions like the UN and bankrupt them using compensation claims. Use empathy laws to push for justice. Charge them for giving the people a false sense of security. For imitating an organization that is supposed to stop wars when they have no enforcement to declare that they can stop wars. For distracting victims as they steal opportunities for the victims to run away. Look at the difference between African refugee wars where the UN plays minor roles and middle east ones. They help facilitate a let no one escape scorched policy as refugees have no time to escape as they give them a false sense of security that they are bombed in their homes whereas Africans would have chances to escape due to the lack of UN to communicate or establish basis in their countries than say in middle east oil-rich countries.

Drag NATO leaders also for breach of empathy laws. We can't say racism acts for the reasons given above but empathy laws can sink them. They authorised the killings through article 5 blanket license to kill others. For doing nothing, look at the 2003 war. In most cases, it is the same countries outsourcing terror to justify military action see the 1960 U2 saga.

Drag to court for genocide. They are deliberately killing blacks; greying them when they complain publicly about racism labelling them as mentally ill and greying their hair. This a way they claim to warn their people that the people are crazy. A way to hide racism and torture abuse. A way to hide the use of child soldiers who are hacked at birth and controlled remotely to be groomed by the police, hospitals, and the council as prostitutes to trap men who are threats to the monarchy, etc. See the CIA's use of prostitutes to hack and kill their targets. A way to trap celebrities and then the NHS use radiation on them to drive say cancer medicines etc. campaigns. Not all are but most are. They are using or will use Covid to hack more then go on to use GPS to link these and ambush them using the police to kill blacks to justify their existence. See defunding of the police as we are arguing that these institutions are obsolete. Go to the Netherlands: all jobs they used to do are legalised. Cannabis is legal to smoke. No speed limits. Burglars are sophisticated and steal from cryptocurrencies rather than banks. That leaves them with nothing to do but be delegated to --all mass hacked people to further abuse or pretend to offer protection then get them ambushed. Look at the killings of innocent kids or by mistake by these. Most are hacked with the hospital using GPS to set them up wrongly so that the police kill them 'accidentally'. If all the killings are accidental for sure, THEN IT FOLLOWS ALSO THAT THEY ARE INCOMPETENT to protect anyone and must cease to do so.

They are using advanced technology to hack people and still do the prohibited secret five

techniques of torture. Digitally hooding people pulling the iris-pupil behind the socket so people can't see.

The hospital because the police have no jobs as everything is now legalised creates jobs for them by breaching international laws etc. The very reason they can't fight the abusive doctors despite some getting struck off. These are their bosses. Creating work for them through illegal hacking and waiting 6 months until no court challenges can be made or accepted by the courts. Need for a change in the law. No time limits to all cases. Above all, they make the courts very expensive money-making machines rather than. Justice systems. A change of the court systems sees our court systems. Sanctions and boycott against torture using Britain.

Issuing of the Ultima-talionis letters. Our license to kill by approved assassins who will work for us after licensing guns globally. A perfect enforcement system so the law is abided by everyone. If the courts fail the assassins can always do a better job.

Peace to all mankind regardless of colour, social status, or orientation politically or sexually. AND FREE MEANS FREE IN THE REAL MEANING OF THE WORD.

No secret commanding and abusing most hacking is done for the sexual gratification of the police, hospitals, and council staff who with the joy sticks abuse the victims by passing static electricity through their genitals remotely and then giving the victims as gifts to other people e.g. celebrities. These are people in a position of trust we are talking about.

They are ageing blacks faster as well using these devices wrinkling them faster, shaking and creasing their faces destroying people. Then grey their hairs then take their kids away or prohibit mating with their own as a population control thing.

So many things to address.

TRUST ME WE ARE THE ONLY SOLUTION. ASK ME WHY? This is the first time you might have heard of a complete change of the system and introduction a new system that is feared and adhered to by everyone. IF THERE WAS A SOLUTION OUT THERE SINCE IT HAS BEEN 75 YEARS since the current system was fully operational BY NOW SURELY A SOLUTION WOULD HAVE BEEN FOUND. The fact that the problems then are the problems now means there are no solutions but Tomorrow's World Order's ladies and gentlemen Welcome to Tomorrow's World Order.

War is a final solution when all countries target the culprit country and attack until the country is sunk.

Founder and president David Gomadza signed
15 November 2020

5 CHAPTER NAME

PART 2

20/11/2022, 22:52 Mail - david gomadza - Outlook
**Evidential Information regarding the submitted case: Part2
Who is behind the pandemic and the Fire/War to Follow? Part
1 Who is really behind the Nazi-led Holocaust?? The truth will
shock you??**
david gomadza <davidgomadza@hotmaiI.com>
Tue 11/3/2020 11:23 PM
To: mailbox.ypp@hq.nato.int
<mailbox.ypp@hq.nato.int>;wma@wma.net <wma@wma.net>
Cc: public@asean.org <public@asean.org
>;unodaviennaoffice@unvienna.org
<unodaviennaoffice@unvienna.org>
PART 2
WHO IS BEHIND THE CURRENT PANDEMIC AND THE
FIRE OR WAR TO FOLLOW???

Main aim: Since it started in China if man-made then a population
control and overcrowding thing. A way to take back money from
the people. Money governments believe that people took out using
digital currencies from the economy's circulation. A government's
clever way of introducing new barbaric laws. And a new way of
getting away with mass murder. Since they all use the mirroring
technique. This can also greatly benefit England and even the USA
and the whole world, mainly the first world countries against
recent migrations to their countries.
BLACK DEATH 1665-1666 GREAT FIRE. Cleansing of
London/England and globally (Watch the rise of killings by police
and the racial protests just this year-- DELIBERATE KILLINGS-
BLACK DEATH) of blacks after exiting the Eurozone. (Reference
1665 Bubonic plague and the black death). A case of genocide or
mass murder.

COULD THERE BE A FIRE OR WAR ON BLACKS ETC ON THE CARDS AS A FIRE ALWAYS FOLLOWS A HARD-TO-BEAT PANDEMIC?

First, I will look at the great fire of London of 1666 that happened soon after the 1665 bubonic plague. This is because you must know the main actors, the kings, and other people at the time as the Documented Great plague of 1665 does not fully show the rulers and those in power directly.

1665 1666 THE GREAT PLAGUE OF ENGLAND AND THE GREAT FIRE OF LONDON. CAST RELIVING THE LIVES OF THE PEOPLE AT THE TIME.
James II of England played by. Guess who? Look alike. TODAY'S LEADER?

https://outlook.live.com/mail/0/id/AQQkADAwATZiZmYAZC1m
NTUAOS1iMDQxLTAwAi0wMAoAEADZorJWn2yUTZF8FMu
vBLh6

King Charles II was king during the GREAT PLAGUE OF LONDON of 1665 and the GREAT FIRE OF LONDON of 1666.

China....where it all started... outbreak of coronavirus---?? John Evelyn played by ...Guess who?
 Predicted the fire? Wrote in his diary or book.
John Evelyn had big dreams for the city/country has already drawn up plans for the city before the fire. The time fire occurred during the Great Fire of London of 1666 he ran to the Queen and offered his plans for the new city whilst the fire was still burning.
ONE THING TO NOTE ABOUT THE NEXT CHARACTER IS THAT HE IS THE INVENTOR OF INTERVENTION
DRUG ADMINISTRATION USING NEEDLES.
Wren's early experiments established the baseline for the invention of intravenous therapy.
Transfusion of blood between animals followed in 1659, eventually leading
     transfusions between sheep and men a practice that became fashionable the

1660s.
https://hekint.org/2019/12/03/christopher-wren-and-blood-circulation/

Christopher Wren was an architect at the time designing the new map of London the same plan used for the development of the new city called New York in America named after James II King Charles II's brother. Making London and New York twin cities. Meaning using the twins mirroring image notion. WHATEVER HAPPENS IN LONDON MUST HAPPEN IN NEW YORK. His designs/ideas are the ones used for the construction of the 9/11 Twin Towers and guess who
bought the twin towers just before the 2001 attacks? LARRY SILVERSTEIN. Now, this is the shock. Whatever this Christopher Wren wanted; the destruction of London so that he can construct new buildings without paying huge compensation claims etc. which he was pleased by the fire. Going to king Charles II and his brother James II offering them New Plans for London as the fires ravaged. This is exactly what the man who RE-LIVED his life- LARRY SILVERSTEIN wanted and did as the twin towers tumbled during 9/11. BUT THE SHOCK IS IN THE RESEMBLANCE to cast doubt altogether of all this being a coincidence.
Ladies and gentlemen meet CHRISTOPHER WREN AND THE MAN WHO RE-LIVED HIS LIFE LARRY SILVERSTEIN.
Colony/Society Collapse Strategy.
Christopher Wren in his studies of the bees in 1654. Developed a strategy that was later used to control people who revolted. His studies of bees made him observe that when the male bees were isolated, separated, or removed eventually the bee colonies would self-destruct in the end. In that, the left males will not take the roles left vacant by the missing males. Unable to feed themselves or even eat the young male bees die too. But the greatest impact was the isolation of males and putting them in see-through glass houses based on the bees see through glass containers proposed by Christopher Wren. The main origin of the ideas behind the Guantanamo cages is that are see-through. A psychological manipulation technique that diffuses any acts of uprising and accusations of wrongdoing as people will instinctively perceive

that everything was okay. As people who are held against all international laws are abused in public. The fact that they are not hidden somewhere secret but in open-see-through-glasses raises less criticism even though it is bad enough. The worst part is the resulting HUMAN-HACKING as Christopher Wren puts it, replacing white sugar with honey-- digital miniature plane parts rotary propellers, GPS, black boxes, etc. all in miniature sizes even the size of the grain. Most are secretly implanted when people are asked to be tested but these are instead implanted to cause the signs of symptoms etc. through remote electromagnetic nerve stimulation and tampering using drone technology. This is the end OF ALL HUMAN RIGHTS- as the coronavirus or outbreak will be used to hack other races. The trick is that everything is digitized with prominent people getting all symptoms to drive their causes to soften the targets. Getting all humans hacked and then using the hacking devices to cause the 'Great Fires' or deaths of most blacks or other people.

Nevertheless, an attempted mass murder and or mass murder if this happens. (30/10/2020). ALSO RELATED TO 9/11

READ THIS BOOK TOO I WROTE THIS BOOK (Pen name Carolinadeivid) https://www.amazon.co.uk/Vice-President-Electronic-Transfer-Death- ebook/dp/B07N4116LB/ref= mp_s_a_1_7?

dchild= 1&keywords=carolinadeivid&qid=1604037366&sr=8-7

https://www.amazon.co.uk/Vice-President-Electronic-Transfer/dp/1793114358

This Christopher Wren was the first person to use gunpowder to demolition or destroy buildings as building demolitions in the 1600s with some during 9/11 pointing to an inside job as thermite or gunpowder was believed to have caused the buildings of the Twin Towers to collapse rather than office fires of paper and wood.

The same person who developed a Timeball.

A device secretly used to predict the fall of something. In this case, the stock markets tipping those who know about this on 11 September 2001 to invest in stock markets and take out money just before the collapse in 2008 see below. Tower three of the world trade centre FREE FELL 6.6 seconds. Those who knew about Timeball could calculate precisely when the markets would fall. 11 September 2001 plus 6.6 years is EXACTLY May 2008 the exact time or soon after of the GLOBAL FINANCIAL COLLAPSE. Find out who benefited the most and from which countries. Check unusual deposits or withdrawals etc. A Timeball is therefore a device to calculate time placed on top of a roof. A device that was used to predict and calculate the free fall of a huge ball placed on top of a roof to determine the exact time to be used by ship captains of 6.6 seconds. At the exact time, 7 seconds the Third Tower of the world trade centre fell. The idea of the Timeball was used to demolish the third world centre as the Timeball or roof with the levers and centre pillar was pulled down with the third world trade centre free falling.

The collapse of New York's World Trade Centre on September 11, 2001 is arguably one of the most well-documented events in human history. Less well documented is the controversy over why the buildings fell as they did. At the time of writing, 357 architectural and engineering professionals have signed a petition which directly challenges the National Institute of Standards & Training's official finding that the destruction of these massive buildings was caused solely by structural damage from the impact of jet airliners and the resulting fires.

https://amp.abc.net.au/article/31852
Robert Hooke played by Rudy Gulliani during 9/11
Robert Hooke was; A **polymath** (Greek:
noZuga0rjq, *polymathés,* "having learned much"; Latin: *homo universal,* "universal man)'1! is an individual whose knowledge spans a significant number of subjects, known to draw on complex bodies of knowledge to solve specific problems.

In the great fire of London Robert Hooke was the centre of the clean-up operations amidst the

1. **Just like Ruby Giuliani after the 9/11 attacks.**

THE ONLY THING THAT CONCERNS ME IS THE FACT THAT innocent people are getting killed when whoever is behind this-'--- the hospitals, police, and doctors who act as film directors using sirens (not to be confused with the sirens due to the

pandemic cases) hacking humans illegally and then directs them to RELIVE other people's lives. (DOCUMENTED CASES) Recreate everything and
choosing the actors who resemble the people concerned and DOING exactly as that person did is a cause of concern. WE ARE FOR THE NEW SYSTEM IN THE FUTURE.
We are against going back to the past for today's solutions recreating past events for two main reasons.
1. We believe that before this pandemic these professions were and are still OBSOLETE. If left unchecked they are going to do what is happening now.
2. Recreating scenes when they first come into existence to remain viable. Create digital viruses to recreate past plagues e.g. the black death of 1665. Triggering wars etc. The police deliberately killing innocent black people etc. to explain the black death or the rise of epidemics or just to recreate and take everyone back to the 1960 - 1980s civil rights movements that marked their highest points.
3. Breaking all international laws takes people back to the dark times when they violated human rights.

6 CHAPTER NAME

We don't care why they are doing it. Murder.

I mean mass murder is still murder and a crime. We don't want to wait years from now as in previous cases to discover that all along this was preplanned and they are following a manual. All calls of prediction etc. are a result of the fact that whoever predicts that. Is tricked into believing that he had foresight. Because as I have illustrated above. We have "film directors" who don't know when to stop and who abuse and trample on other people's lives. Killing innocent people to clean up their nations of other races using methods from the dark ages when mankind was ravaged by diseases etc.

WE ARE THE FUTURE AND CHOOSE NEW WAYS OF THINKING hence our emphasis on a new system led by the political party I founded called TOMORROW'S WORLD ORDER. Even if there is doubt about the accuracy of my analyses, look at the deaths of black people at the hands of law enforcement. Would this not be explained by this analysis? Look at the race riots of 2020. It's like taking us back to the 1960-1980s.

What if the current pandemic is a manmade digital pathogen? A weapon to kill and commit mass murders even worse by those inflicted by the Holocaust. What if it's a way to get people hacked and for them to justify human hacking? Which we know is illegal and can't be justified in any way reason the penalty carries three life sentences. What if this is just the beginning of a DELIBERATE COLONY COLLAPSE STRATEGY to recreate 1654's ideas that saw the glass or fence Guantanamo bay cages and the recorded abuse and violations of human rights? Ideas created by an English polymath Christopher Wren?

The current courts are not equipped to consider these crimes. We are not saying that whoever killed people e.g. Hitler etc. is innocent no. BUT WE ARE SAYING THAT THESE ARE JUST THE SYMPTOMS the actual problem is the system and whoever recreates these.

You might argue that history repeats itself!!

But look at the images and resemblances of the people in time and those that do the same thing.
IT IS NOT A COINCIDENCE BUT A PRE-CALCULATED COLD PLAN TO KILL. Where whoever is
behind this goes back in the past and sees what the problems were then. As related to now. Then like a doctor prescribes the solution then. Then RECREATE the solutions to solve today's problems. No wonder we are stuck in stage 2 of the development process when we should be in stage 4 or 5.
Read. Tomorrow's World
Order https://www.amazon.co.uk/gp/aw/d/B07XTK3N8N/ref=tm m kin title 0? ie=UTF8&qid=1604049071&sr=8-7

Please, this is so lame. But also, a crime under international law. So, we strongly believe that someone out there is or are our suspects being the hospitals, doctors, the leaders, and the police. The four main culprits in all mass killings every time they work together.
(With the doctors hacking everyone illegally, therefore, creating work for the police, etc. As hacked people can be blinded by the devices to prevent them from seeing as the eye pupil is hidden behind the socket e.g. while driving etc. If there is an accident, then they must work. Do you think they will ask the doctors why they hacked and technologically hooded blind digitally the driver? Or they will say thank you to the hospitals and doctors who are using technology GPS black boxes and human hacking to set up police officers to wrongfully kill innocent people.
To make things worse it is you the people paying taxes used to fund these people. Meaning buying whatever they are doing to you as your money funds them. Ever heard of funding terrorists? The very reasons why judge on earth will find them guilty. All the time they will be acquitted simply because the judges will use the reasonable test that no reasonable money will pay up taxes knowing that it funds the very same people who are going to kill them or torture them. As this is like a self-inflicted wound because no reasonable man would pay salaries for people who are going to kill them.
That is why we are calling for a new system that doesn't link taxes to their incomes. We ban taxes altogether. But still, deduct money

from wages and salaries as deposits to their Government-held savings accounts. One they will have access to when they reach a certain age, or the balance has reached a certain amount. We don't fund terrorists in the strictest meaning too. What has happened in 2020 is like them fighting to take the title from the terrorists we know. BUT THE SYSTEM IS DESIGNED for them to do that as now their acts have triggered the mass demonstrations and rise of BlackLivesMatter NOW JUSTIFIES THEIR ACTS as self-preservation act. BUT WE CAN'T BE FOOLED WE KNOW WHAT STARTED FIRST THE EGG OR THE CHICKEN. Hence our calls to

stop paying taxes globally and to reform and upgrade all these professions and DEFUND THE POLICE and better fund homeless projects etc. trigger the problems they are to solve. Mind you their system is based on a pyramid that requires more people at the bottom to justify and support the numbers at the top otherwise it will collapse. FACT!

OUR SYSTEM IS A DIAMOND SHAPE WITH MOST OFF-POVERTY LINE bringing wealth to all.)

HOLOCAUST - the police round the people and order them to be sent to concentration camps for doctors on behalf of hospitals to do experiments on the people. Revisit the Nuremberg trials.

GREAT PLAGUES- to justify the number of police hospitals etc. as the system is a pyramid, they withheld funding from the people. Or they had no cash as in the case of CHARLES II of England in 1665 or keeping money for war instead of feeding the people. That tricked the plague. Just like poverty today.

I argued in my book Tomorrow's World Order Dealing with threats of invasions, sanctions, and intimidations that they are using TIME CAMPS instead of concentration camps BUT WITH THE SAME INTENDED RESULTS: mass murder. Time in that they are withholding funds from the system to trigger mass starvation. Keeping money in war chests with military cults or World Banks, IMF, etc. waiting for the pandemic to do the rest. The mass killings. A new concealed mass murder synonymous with the holocaust only that now they use.

1. Human-hacking and airplane parts black boxes, rotary propellers, GPS tracking, etc. in miniature sizes the size of a thumbnail.

2. Digital weapons or pathogens using electromagnetic nerve tampering and remote-control using drone technology.

3. Making new laws to quarantine and hold people from breaking all laws that existed. Taking people back to the Hitler era only that now it's undetected and in the name of protection of people from the pandemic etc. but surely a man-made digital weapon only that the time you will know the truth it will be too late. They will have covered their tracks.

4. The critical fact is that all those involved who are playing the lives of previous people DON'T EVEN KNOW THAT THIS IS HAPPENING IN THAT THEY WILL DEFEND THEMSELVES AT ANY COST. But

We know that lightning doesn't strike twice at the same spot. But when that happens you can find us asking questions like now! CONSPIRACY OR A DENIAL OF THE TRUTH??? YOU DECIDE.

Our system will never harm innocent people or regard women and children as collateral or even other races as such.

FIRST, WE DON'T BELIEVE IN RACISM IN THE SENSE IT WAS 400 YEARS AGO.

1. These people have gone so far unchallenged because they are waiting for everyone to say its racism and start riots, so they are justified in brutally killing innocent people. FACT. IT IS AN EGG OR CHICKEN QUESTION. A BOOBY TRAP SO THEY ARE JUSTIFIED IN DOING EXACTLY WHAT WE

ARE SAYING IS WRONG. So, they are justified in using the Colony Collapse Strategy that blacks are threats. What else do you expect? Look at the demonstrations they are doing if we don't make these digital pathogens control them it's either us or them.

2. If you are black if you cry racism, they say it is a mental disorder, so they racially abuse that person. But blame it on the condition they will or have already created through human hacking; continuous shaking of the brain (We have proof on video of human hacking that can be provided on request. A hint on all abolished practices speaking of secret slavery, genocide, torture, and secret TIME-not-CONCENTRATION camps of the holocaust. NB. A hacker's aim, be it in computer or human circles, is to cause the MALFUNCTION of otherwise perfect systems. In most cases the plane parts (probably the message of 9/11 attackers a message

that they are killing a race using plane parts. We might never know) the rotary propellers they use to help their aged and old people with liver dysfunction to pump urine etc. from the liver they use the same to shake the brain and damage it so that in the end the person has brain damage. PICTURE A COIN WITH TWO SIDES SO AS THE ROTARY PROPELLERS ON WHITES THEY USE THEM TO IMPROVE THE HEALTH OF BLACKS THEY USE THEM TO DO BRAIN DAMAGE but this could be the same technology. WE HAVE PROOF OF THIS A VIDEO SHOWING BEYOND DOUBT WHAT THEY ARE DOING.

To close that race loophole, we are going to introduce the E-LAWS.

THE EMPATHY LAWS do not rely on race as in racism but on the sole fact that if it was a person close to the culprit, he or she would not have done the same thing. I always use the example of a soldier; a sniper who is about to take out an enemy but only stops shooting when he discovers that the enemy was a boy the same age as his son. Only because of this similarity he disobeyed the command. The next soldier with no kids, pulled the trigger because the boy had a gun therefore regarded as a combatant. The same soldiers have different circumstances and outcomes as well.

7 CHAPTER NAME

So, to conclude for now.

We argue that they are using the mirror image twin techniques of recreating things that happened in the past and the BEST PART IS THAT ALL THIS IS DOCUMENTED WITH REAL IMAGES AND PORTRAITS OF THE PAST PEOPLE WHOSE LIVES THEY ARE MEANT TO LIVE. As a way of finding solutions to current problems.

To know who?? LOOK AT THE PROBLEM AT HAND.

1. 1665-1666

England was on its knees at war in 1665 Second Anglo-Dutch war. All money was used for the war with king Charles II having no money at all.

2. Overcrowding and poor building standards were a problem that architects like Christopher Wren and John Evelyn had already drawn new plans for London even before the fire started. Hinting at a deliberate cause of the fire even though the fire started in the bakery. But would you be surprised after the Great Plague of the same year with 100 000 dying in 18 months? With corpses laying around in the streets. With carts full of people moved all the time. Diseases were rife and all this was attributed to rodents and overcrowding etc. So only fire was a solution. King Charles II even ran away from the city. So, whether deliberate or not the fire was everyone's solution.

3. Today's issues I don't know if people are preparing for World War Three or The Great Fire of some kind to put money in a war chest. But I know cryptocurrency has taken money out of the system. That also made me think that cryptocurrencies are the people's way of taking money out of the system and empowering the people. Coronaviruses are a government direct challenge to the cryptocurrencies of taking money also out of the system as A DIRECT RESPONSE. We don't want to wait for years and to find out that all this was man-made when millions are dead by then. The very reason why Tomorrow's World Order arose in the first place. We are proactive.

To know who is behind all this. WE LOOK AT THE PROBLEM AT HAND.

1. Globally the rise of digital currencies has meant reduced circulating money and money going to the government etc. Imagine all these years before digital currencies governments held more money than the people. The last year 2019 saw a rise in digital currency deposits among the people. Triggering fears of giving the people power, especially in China where the pandemic originated evidenced by the government's crackdown on cryptocurrencies. So, the only government response that can change this and shift the balance of power is a pandemic like the one going on. Instead of bitcoin people are more likely to keep money with them. Less and less work etc. It triggers fears that people might need the cash fast so keep the money as ready liquid cash rather than as bitcoin etc. Overcrowding?? Now the pandemic is used to space out people limiting the number in hotels etc. All this suits China with overcrowding and high population growth rates.

But the situation favours Britain too as they just came out of Euro. Overcrowding and all poor standards are reminiscent of London in 1665. The fact that the government reacted late can make them suspects too. Or they saw an opportunity and took it. Doing exactly as after the 1665 to 1666 plague and fire to introduce new laws that break other laws only as part of the COLONY COLLAPSE STRATEGY rather than a pandemic solution. This is in response to the Racial related riots of 2020.

Picture Christopher Wren's ideas as the chief architect at the time into play here with glass see-through quarantine being contaminants etc. with everyone illegally hacked without consent and secretly as part of the test to check for the pandemic but implanted with things that they will use with digitally made pathogens that imitate the disease in question??

THE BIG QUESTION OR THING FOR ALL OF YOU TO LOOK OUT FOR IS THE GREAT FIRE. One to come after the pandemic to clean up all this.

Hinting at mass killings of mainly blacks check numbers in England and killings of Chinese or other races too in China as well as a way of population control or cleansing the system.

REMEMBER THE TWIN MIRRORING TACTIC.
The question is who and who will be twins?

All said in good faith to stop this if it's manmade and pave the way for a new system that is fair and fit for purpose. A system that takes humanity to the next stage of development away from the defensive stages we are in. Where your leaders with the few resources they have make WEAPONS and then use the weapons to get everything at gunpoint. Things they can't afford. Most often going back in the past to find solutions to DOCUMENTED similar problems. A poor way of solving problems killing innocent people thinking they can get away with it. Not anymore. Our system will raise living standards to levels never thought of before. Bringing wealth to all mankind forever. Welcome to Tomorrow's World Order your Honour, ladies, and gentlemen.
Sincerely
David Gomadza 20 October 2020

From: david gomadza <davidgomadza@hotmail.com> Sent: Friday, October 30, 2020, 2:40 AM
To: mailbox.ypp@hq.nato.int <mailbox.ypp@hq.nato.int>
Subject: Who is really behind Nazi-led Holocaust?? The truth will shock you.

8 CHAPTER NAME

PART 1.
(DOCUMENTED)Edict of expulsion (legal government
document) of the year 1290 of 18 July 1290 By King Edward 1 of
Britain. Persecution of Jews in Britain started from 1019
Look at similarities to Adolf Hitler's acts.
**RELIVING SOMEONE'S LIFE AND MADE TO DO
EXACTLY LIKE THAT PERSON.**
Like a movie. Following documented written scripts. Directed just
like in a Hollywood movie following history as the script.
This is the proof.
Ladies and gentlemen Adolf Hitler playing KING EDWARD 1 OF
ENGLAND doing everything he did from making decrees to fight
the Jews to living his life. Formally making the Edict of Expulsion
into law on 18 July 1290 and cleaning England of the Jews.
It does not stop there he lives his life as well in the photos or
portraits done to resemble those of the man whose life he is living.
He went on to live his life too and got a woman Eva Braun who
resembled or looked like Eleanor king Edward 1's wife. Look at
the portraits with Eva that resemble Edward 1 king of England
with Eleanor.
Now recall the hatred of the Jews etc. exactly like this king of
England.
So, if King Edward 1 of England got away from doing the same
thing. Surely I can only assume and note that I am NOT siding
with anyone but the fact that a British king did the same thing and
did not get punished meant probably that he did not expect anyone,
especially the British to attack him. Unless they were behind all
this all along planned and after he gave them an alibi covering their
king, they moved in to silence him and get rid of the evidence
having covered their king's actions.
So, if they saw it fit to attack him the same if their king was alive
was to be attacked as well by all countries. First, I profusely am
against all barbaric acts and killings. So, our stance is that he could
simply say he was highlighting an open case of the holocaust

45

against King Edward 1. The fact that his acts went unpunished therefore unless he is punished first then justice hasn't been done. So, whatever he did he was tricked - tortured and driven to extremes by torture to do those things as they wanted an alibi for their rotten king. So again, was their king clean? All cases therefore must first be looked at ...The reason is that this act is common and regarded as a sacrifice. Where kings commit the worst crimes and document in black and white everything then ask innocent people to do the same. To protect the king in that the person covers the evil acts of the king. But this is 2020 the king must fall too. The only way to close these holocaust cases is before anyone can even think about healing and forgiving. This is my initial personal view. It is just too much to be a coincidence.

Below Edward 1's portrait from 1239 to his end of reign as King in 1307
Bottom Adolf Hitler's photo. LOOK AT THE RESEMBLANCE with above Edward 1's photo. MAKES IT HARD TO BRUSH ASIDE THE IDEA OF ALL THIS BEING PREPLANNED. Note we are not exonerating anyone but are saying there are other players.

Above Edward 1 (Adolf Hitler, temporarily blinded by a British gas shell and evacuated to a German military hospital at Pasewalk, in Pomerania.)

King Edward 1 (above) and
King Edward 8 (below with & Hitler

Expulsion of Jews Adolf Hilter and Nazi with Edward Duke of Windsor former king of Britain.

Edward viii is a decoy for Edward 1 of 1290. Who issued the EDICT OF EXPULSION of 18 July 1290 that removed and persecuted all Jews from Britain? The resemblance of Adolf Hitler to Edward 1 is astonishing and the basis of the theory is that if the photo of Edward 1 is a portrait then we can only conclude that people with the same gene makeup might as a probability do and

feel the same way. Looking alike means having similar genes
(even though twins might act differently) there is a chance of them
behaving the same way or being easily influenced to act like the
former. Or knowing in advance that he might do like the former
but if they go on to abuse even their secrets that rules out this
possibility.
King Edward 1 of Britain issued a decree against Jews and used
the constables / the police to expel all.
Edict of Expulsion of 1290.
Hitler does the same- issued the final solution to deal with the Jews
after they came back to Europe after being expelled by King
Edward 1. That starts the torture and persecution of the Jews.
Now killing and sending all to concentration camps.
Even then the British were the first to use concentration camps on
the Boers of South Africa in the meaning the word we know today
even though they say the Spanish did the same.
     Face south.
Position Edward viii and Hitler check which direction. IF
CORRECT THEY ARE FACING TOWARD SALZBURG IN
AUSTRIA or near there.
(All this a secret language that uses MIRRORING of some sort to
give or explain things without saying it, especially if scared that
someone else might be listening.)

Before tea," the New York Times reported, "Hitler showed his
guests (Edward
VIII) the house and grounds. They stood for some time on the
terrace looking down into Austria, with the border town of
Salzburg framed between the mountains down into Austria, with
the border town of Salzburg
A reference to the British use of the Concentration camp in
Rhodesia Salisbury. This is
1 37 by ig3 He is using the same tactics of concentration camps???
Salisbury=Capital of Rhodesia SOUTH AFRICA BOERS OF
SOUTH AFRICA. Robert Cecil, earl of Salisbury, also called
(•59*—i6o3) Sir Robert Cecil, or (from 16o3) Baron Cecil of
Essendon, or (from 16O4) Viscoun
The British fought the Boers for the mines rather than protect
oppressed Africans. When they were using the Scorched Earth

Policy. So, the fight was to control the gold mines of Transvaal South Africa rather than fighting the Boers because they oppressed non-Boers in South Africa. They secretly torture non-whites in 2020 in their country so talk of liberating these doesn't hold water. The aim was to control the gold mines.

So, the salt mines of Berchtesgaden Germany hinted at the gold mines of South Africa. Meaning how best to protect these by putting all in concentration camps and letting hunger and disease kill all from 1899 to 1902 as the British did with the Boers.

My argument is that they saw an opportunity and took it and let Hitler re-live the life of their King

Edward 1 to cleanse his evil acts. No wonder they were at the forefront. The truth was not because of the need to liberate Jews or the Polish no but for the gold mines- VAST GOLD DATA OF ALL THE HUMAN EXPERIMENTS CARRIED OUT BY THE NAZIS so they can build even more secret hidden technologically advanced miniature weapons of torture. Etc.

I think you need to look more at this 1290 Edict of Expulsion and the persecution and relate it to what happened during the Holocaust.

Again, I am not saying that Hitler did not do anything wrong, but these countries are still doing the same thing but hidden secretly through human hacking and remote nerve tampering. Using drone software undetected.

I will send more information.

The fact that their king does the same and gets away with it means it was a take-over and getting rid of the evidence rather than a liberation. Surely you don't expect a killer of women and children to stand up for women and children considering their king expelled and killed the Jews. How will they stand up for the Jews? I raised this issue because they keep using torture and all forbidden methods. The Nuremberg trials changed the Germans. It is the countries that got away still at the forefront. I lived in Germany. Documented evidence that its government stance is against Semitism even though not officially. There is a general feeling of antisemitism in the UK as well as all over the world, but these are documented and influential to ignore.

Getting Jesus killed is not enough for those who committed the greatest sin to walk away. Note that.
WHATEVER THEY ACCUSE OTHERS OF DOING. THEY ARE ONLY COVERING FOR THEIR KING etc.
They say holocaust-- look at their kings they might have done worse.
Abuse of women and children-- again look at them first, their kings, etc. they might have done worse and set up others to cover for them.
Whatever they accuse others there is usually documented evidence of their kings having done worse and
to show power then set up a person and then sacrifice that person to clear their kings.
If you want justice, it starts with these. They point fingers and then look at them first.
Look at women and children killed using the Scorched Earth Policy. If they can do that, they can't be expected to care for anyone.
Now they use torture secretly and pretend its others making noises etc. the reason for complaining etc. To cover their tracks but fortunately end up understanding their secrets as well. Crimes are crimes especially if they are the worst crimes in history then they must be fully investigated. Just a few months ago a 93-year-old man was tried for the Holocaust crimes and for the first time a person was found to be guilty even though they did not directly participate. We take the same stance Only because they are using SECRET TORTURE a tortured person is like a hostage at gunpoint in that whatever he or she does is at the gun point it could be that he was forced or tricked and such cases must be investigated until there is no doubt whatsoever. Then we can start talking about peace and forgiveness. The only way to a peaceful future without revenge attacks.
Sincerely
David Gomadza
26 October 2020
October 30, 2020 2:40 AM

9 CHAPTER NAME

To: mailbox.ypp@hq.nato.int <mailbox.ypp@hq.nato.int>
Subject: Who is really behind the Nazi-led Holocaust?? The truth will shock you??

tomorrow's World Order
Global Political Party
tomorrowsworldorder@outlook.com
05/01/2021
The International Criminal Court
Information and Evidence Unit
Office of the Prosecutor
Post Office Box 19519
2500 CM The Hague
The Netherlands or sent by email to otp.informationdesk@icc-cpi.int or sent by facsimile to +31 70 515 8555.
Dear Your Honorable.
THE CASE OF TOMORROW'S WORLD ORDER vs THE LEADERS OF THE WORLD OF ALL COUNTRIES ON EARTH WHO HAVE IMPOSED AND FORCED LOCKDOWN RESTRICTIONS AND ENFORCED THESE IN RESPONSE TO THE COVID PANDEMIC OF 2020-2021 THAT RESULTED IN MORE DEATHS DURING AND SOON AFTER THAT. [SEE EVIDENCE 1, 2,3]
1. ROME STATUTE OF THE INTERNATIONAL CRIMINAL COURT
2. Part 2.
3. JURISDICTION, ADMISSIBILITY, AND APPLICABLE LAW
*Article 51 Crimes within the jurisdiction of the Court. The jurisdiction of the Court shall be limited to the **most serious crimes of concern to the international community**. The Court has jurisdiction in accordance with this Statute with respect to the following crimes: [Emphasis added].*
4. (b) Crimes against humanity.

*5. c)CRIMES AGAINST HUMANITY: namely, [mass] **murder,
extermination**, enslavement, deportation, and other inhumane acts
committed against any civilian population, before or during the
war;* [crime against humanity can also be committed in
peacetime.] *or persecutions on political, racial or religious
grounds in the execution of or in connection with any crime within
the jurisdiction of the Tribunal, whether or not in violation of the
domestic law of the country where perpetrated.*
6. Leaders, organizers, instigators, and accomplices *participating
in* **the formulation or execution of a common plan or conspiracy
to commit any of the foregoing crimes are responsible for all acts
performed by any persons in the execution of the such plan.**
**7. That includes everyone including the local police of all
countries and the hospitals who might be helping them enforce
and carry out all these.**
8. We as Tomorrow's World Order argue that a lot of things have
changed since these statutes were implemented and we want the
court to look at these issues in light of the changing environment
and amend these regardless of the **gravity of the crimes** as they
threaten the fabric of human existence.
9. A *reasonable basis* to initiate an investigation in the interest of
justice. Pandemic.
Total cases
85.9M
Recovered
48.3M
Deaths
1.86M

10. As at 05/01/2021.
11. Failings and creation of conditions that fuel the virus are not
only evils but fall under crimes against humanity murder
meaning **mass murder** and or genocide to some extent areas the
court has jurisdiction to act upon. 12. WHAT ARE CRIMES
AGAINST HUMANITY?
*13. Crimes against humanity refer to specific crimes committed in
the context of a **large-scale attack targeting civilians, regardless***

*of their nationality. These crimes include murder, torture, sexual violence, enslavement, persecution, enforced disappearance, etc. Crimes against humanity have **often been committed as part of State policies**, but they can also be perpetrated by non-State armed groups or paramilitary forces. Unlike war crimes, crime against humanity can also be **committed in peacetime**, and contrary to genocide, they are not necessarily committed against a specific national, ethnic, racial, or religious group.*

14. ICC WEBSITE.

15. These crimes **were committed after 1 July 2002,** the date of the entry into force of the Rome Statute, the Court's founding treaty; the crimes took place in the territory of a State Party or **were committed by a citizen of a State Party**. They **amount to crimes against humanity or genocide; the gravity of these crimes means that they must be investigated asap.**

16. Where the State is the vehicle of persecution and mass murder there is no talk of local or national redress nor investigations and prosecutions as the state itself is the one responsible.

17. [National authorities bear the primary responsibility, in the first instance, to investigate and prosecute those most responsible for the commission of mass crimes. The Court will initiate investigations, in accordance with the legal criteria set by the Rome Statute, only when the national authorities have failed to uphold this primary responsibility and in the absence of genuine national proceedings.]

18. But if they are the ones responsible and ordering the shutdowns then the talk of national redress is non-existence. Therefore, the court is obliged to look at this as this has gone global.

19. We as Tomorrow's World Order believe that there is a criminal intent to kill people deliberately or indirectly. Such reckless acts whether deliberate or due to sheer ignorance cannot be tolerated or left unpunished. We strongly believe that nevertheless how natural the pandemic might seem to people. We strongly believe that there is a malicious criminal intent by these governments and their leaders to kill as many people as they can for the following reasons:

20. To hide evidence of human hacking.

21. To get rid of the so-called 'dead-wood' in the pensioners, people who make most of the government expenses in pensions, etc.

22. A population control mechanism.

23. We strongly believe that the Lockdowns are being enforced too.

24. Weaken the human immune system so that during and immediately after lockdown the virus will do maximum damage and kill as many as the people would have been weakened. 25. Weeks of lockdown even though not the intended plan has the effect of weakening greatly the human immune system that during and soon after lockdown the number of cases will shoot up significantly. See attachment. We think this is the reason for the lockdown. That brings us to the real intention of the lockdowns.

26. Are they deliberately trying to kill as many as they can? Do they have a target number? Say 100 000 in a country like England? This is not speculative; we will give you our basis for suggesting that. See below arguments considering the 1665-1666 England pandemic.

27. We strongly believe that it is well known to all that since this is a viral pandemic ALL PROPOSED AND IMPLEMENTED "SOLUTIONS" HAVE THE EFFECT OF FEEDING THE VIRUS. 28. We believe that if it was a BACTERIAL INDUCED PANDEMIC yes, the solutions including lockdowns "might" have worked. But this is a VIRAL pandemic and all these leaders with a bunch of advisers etc. must know that.

a. Lockdown reduces the body's ability to fight infections.

b. Reduces the body's natural ability to defend itself against viruses.

c. No exercises. Even general walking is cut off by the forced lockdowns and the enforcement. Leaving the body exposed without the protective shield.

d. Lockdowns themselves induce stress that weakens the person. The very reason why they lock people in jails especially those associated with murder or violent crimes. To weaken them in all the meanings of the word.

e. This stress is different from any stress as this takes away the freedoms of the people. Taking away the hope and belief of the day after tomorrow. The hope for the stress of the future to increase. Don't forget these people are already stressed up by the pandemic itself.

f. High stress levels increase the chances of one getting sick.

g. The government's strategy of announcing cases and deaths daily live on national television is to further increase the stress and further weaken the people. The idea is to traumatise people giving them an ever-growing sense of worry and anxiety all of which weakens the natural defence system.

h. We want to make the court aware that we are dealing with clever, devious, and manipulating people. People who will do anything. Who will trick, deceive, and force people to their deaths?

i. The lockdowns are to weaken and kill the self-esteem of the people and their sense of belonging. Carrying out a SCORCHED EARTH POLICY of removing anything that will help people recover from the effects of lockdowns. That is hope. Bonding with friends and relatives. Keeping them in lockdown for more than two weeks could be said to be the maximum a human body can go without severe extremes. This means the intention is to weaken.

j. Lockdowns destroy the greatest weapon a human system can use to boost its immune system. Self Esteem. People on lockdown are just going to sit and eat and feel unattractive and worthless as they become chubby etc. Sitting down and doing nothing will have a negative impact.

k. Lockdowns mean people will spend most of their time indoors, the exact opposite of what they should do as time spent outdoors is cut off.

l. Lockdown stops cooperation and networking that would otherwise boost their confidence and feel-good factors to strengthen their immune system.

29. WE STRONGLY BELIEVE THAT THE APPROACH ADOPTED IS FLAWED. In that, they LOOKED AT THE VIRUS INSTEAD OF THE HUMAN IMMUNE SYSTEM. We believe this is deliberate to have the greatest impact. Meaning killing more. Looking at the virus will only result in these leaders finding ways of avoiding the virus. WE BELIEVE THEY SHOULD HAVE LOOKED AT WAYS TO BOOST THE HUMAN IMMUNE SYSTEM.

30. Surely if isolation and lockdown will weaken the human immune system as people exercise less. As people worry too much.

As the sources of comfort and boost to self-esteem are restricted e.g. in seeing emotional support in friends and family. Then they would not have proposed and implemented lockdowns. But because they looked at the VIRUS rather than the people's defence system this has become a THIRD-TYPE ERROR. Yes, they have solutions but for a different or wrong problem. They are doing something but it's all wrong in this case. Fuelling the pandemic and deaths.

31. BUT WE BELIEVE IT IS INTENTIONAL AND ALL MUST BE HELD ACCOUNTABLE. This is the very reason why people were put in concentration camps. THE LOCKDOWNS SECRETLY CREATE THE CONDITIONS WHICH WE CALL 'BREEDING GROUNDS FOR THE VIRUS.

32. Yes. This method might have worked if this was a bacterial outbreak. The fact that they all know this makes us bring all 200 plus to you one by one. We know it's a lot of work but that is the very reason why you are there. You have our support all the way. No one is above the law. Send a clear message. To assess and bring all to trial for the following crimes. a. Mass murder depending on circumstances.

b. Holding their citizens as hostages and under indirect house arrest. The enforcement supports this. This is hostage-taking.

c. Forcing their citizens against their will, breaching their human rights, and putting them all at risk of death by weakening them through the forced lockdowns. Humans hack and try to or getting rid of the evidence by forced lockdowns knowing that most are likely to die. We believe this is an attempt to destroy secret human hacking evidence that used to be done secretly. We have proof of human hacking and this is proof too that they might have tried to use the pandemic to bury the hatchet with it.

e. In line with this is that even though the pandemic might have started in China. Some might have killed or are killing their people using digital viruses and electromagnetic nerve tampering in the disguise of the virus using drone technology.

f. Failing to protect their citizens in time of need deliberately or unintentionally. That means a breach of care for these people. They are in power to protect the people. Failure is unacceptable.

g. Ignorance is not an excuse. They have enough people and experts to get the correct information. After one year they should have quizzed the professionals. h. Giving their people a false sense of security that they can protect them, especially the victims when they can't. Bearing in mind that ignorance can't be relied upon due to time limits.

i. Breaching all human rights of these people. Rights to freedom of expression as they are forced to keep silent in lockdowns. Depriving them of rights to freedom of association and holding peaceful associations and demonstrations.

j. Rights not to be held against their wills.

k. Criminalising the victims of the pandemic holding them against their wills and using other conditions to hold them illegal. Number one is under mental health and they will claim that the virus causes mental stress to cover for the stress induced by the lockdowns.

l. Genocide. They are going to claim that the pandemic mainly affects blacks and Asians, generally, people of colour to give themselves an alibi before they use other means to kill and destroy ethnic people. We believe also that they might have used the pandemic to try and cover issues reported to the courts before in relation to genocide, secret modern-day slavery, etc.

m. This brings us to illegal human hacking. They are deliberately human hacking the people. Implanting miniature airplane parts that rotate and damage the brain. So, all this is a cover-up. We have proof of human hacking. FACT.

n. We believe they are carrying out genocide. Destroying the ethnic people using hacking to damage the brain and enslave secretly the people. Greying all as they regard all as suffering from mental health. So, to alert people to grey their hair. It a genocide as they are destroying people and this pandemic is a cover-up. Trying to bury the hatchet with the pandemic.

o. We believe they are suppressing opposition using illegal lockdowns as a means of destroying the financial aspect of the opposition. Scorched Earth Policy. Lockdowns are simply a way of removing resources mainly financial from the people. Lockdown is a way of removing and limiting the power of people. A good example is the strictness of lockdowns in Britain in likely opposition countries namely Scotland and Wales where they might be the hardest hit by the pandemic. It does not matter how and who started the pandemic. They might all have seen an opportunity and taken it globally as well.

p. They are using lockdowns to hold the women and children as bargaining tools. Just like sanctions they are causing suffering to these so their leaders in countries with active opposition submit. Especially where there are no accompanied means of aid, financial resources, or otherwise.

q. The main reason is to weaken all their immune systems as food might be an issue for people on lockdown. As most have now reduced salaries. Fewer hours worked and no ways to claim government support and by the time the lockdowns end they might be in debt. Increasing the possibility of becoming a victim of the virus.

r. We recommend the court use the E-laws here. The empathy laws are if it was someone close to them. A relative etc. would have or might have arrived at a different solution. Instead of lockdowns.

33. To us, as Tomorrow's World Order we believe that the best way is to look at the best way to build the HUMAN DEFENSE SYSTEM NATURALLY.

a. This would have meant.

b. Strengthening the human system. Immune system meaning.

i. No lockdowns but people are allowed to stay outdoors in the open or very well-ventilated places etc.

ii. 24 hours of everything that boosts self-confidence, self-esteem, a sense of building and well-being, that builds the body's strength, places that invigorate, rejuvenate, soothe, comfort, give people a sense of hope, etc. namely.

1. Gyms are open 24 hours. Creating outdoor gyms etc.

2. Places of worship.

3. Hairs dressers as beautifying people would boost self-esteem and give people better chances of developing self-defence against the virus.

4. Beauty therapists.

5. Massage salons and yoga.

6. Fighting clubs for self-defence.

7. Pubs as places for social networking and cooperating.

8. National get-togethers but for exercises, aerobics, etc. not for alcohol consumption or anything that weakens the immune system.

9. Demonstration groups and a sense of national solidarity.

10. Anything else that gives hope.

34. Withdrawing of financial resources at the time of the greatest need. The governments are ignoring the basic needs, choosing to increase military budgets at such a time when the pandemic has ravaged most people. The poorest even in developed countries have become hard hit in some countries with charities taking a leading role to feed the children and women etc. No financial backing for the ordinary people and the governments choose businesses more. Lack of a duty of care towards these people especially women and children.

35. We know during pandemics things can be hard but doing more damage is not only evil but a criminal offence. There are greater expectations from these leaders and there is a need for greater responsibilities. When that fails this not only amounts to incompetence but a crime.

36. We are basing our answers on the fact that this is a viral pandemic and just like any virus illness like the cold. The body will get rid of the virus by itself. No medicines work against the cold virus itself. That is why colds are still here now. All medicines tend only to alleviate the symptoms. So, likewise, everything should have been done to help boost the immune system. They had this knowledge a year ago. They waited. That brings me to another accusation.

1. Procrastinating and waiting for the virus to do maximum damage first before acting and when they did it was the wrong kind of action.

2. These recommendations are in line with the fact that a year has gone, and they are still recording the greatest daily infection and death rates. Surely that means something is wrong. We are not saying that people won't die but we believe in strengthening the people naturally not by limiting movements and exercises which have a direct impact on the immune system and the ability of the body to handle the virus.

3. Lockdowns only make people take longer to develop a natural defence system without vaccines. There would be more cases of the Covid virus but reduced deaths.

4. The adopted method would have fewer Covid cases which also MEANS fewer PEOPLE WHO ARE NATURALLY IMMUNE TO THE virus and more extreme deaths. The very argument of our case. See attached graphs for proof.

5. But by boosting the immune system so the body can naturally defend itself. This would also reduce the length of time before the people recover etc. If this was the plan things could have been better. We can still prevent needless deaths. The vaccines work on the same principle but have huge side effects and costs. Million people have died globally we can't stand and watch these give it a last go and claim many before everything comes to an end when vaccines are finally introduced.

6. We believe that this one last LOCKDOWN push is to do maximum damage to justify huge vaccine purchases when the lockdowns end.

As we believe that there will be huge infections and deaths after the lockdowns for the reasons explained above. It's like a shock and scare for people not to complain tomorrow about governments' waste or delays in doing something beneficial.

37. Another crime is that of the third type of error.

38. Deliberately misleading the people. Pretending to tackle the pandemic but making deals and distributing wealth into the community money that would end up back to their Trusts, legacy organisations, or party politics one day. This is because they will or might deliberately purchase useless e.g. protective gear against the virus. Then pretend it is because of the pandemic meaning lack of time etc. and many will be recommended by their party people or suppliers. They will deliberately choose wrong solutions to scare people as deaths
increase weakening them not to protest but to submit and not point to corruption or misuse of government funds.

39. Lockdowns instead of less time indoors can amount to a criminal offence depending on the number of deaths, duration, and if forced or not. If enforced or not etc.

40. Misuse of government money. All the beneficiaries must be investigated. Links established as to trust, legacies, political parties, etc. All vaccine companies are to be investigated too. 41. The other crime is to apportion blame. Taking advantage of the viruses will make people partly blamed for their creation. If the

plan is to gain unfavourably that means you also have a motive for making or spreading the virus as well therefore a suspect too. This is in line with the thinking that it can be homemade and exported abroad and then waiting for it to roll back so that the end justifies the means. There are issues of colluding too to make the virus and gain as well.

42. Incompetent to protect their people.

43. Incompetent to rule and do things for humanity's protection.

44. Hence the need and justification of us Tomorrow's World Order as the new official global leaders to:

45. Lead, Guide, Oversee, and Rule the world.

46. I have pointed out that some countries recreate the past exactly by putting the same lookalike people then and doing exactly like them. I know this is **controversial,** but it is open to us to ask the court to look at this and rule out criminal acts. We know lightning doesn't strike twice but when it does that leaves us with so many more questions than answers. England's 1665-1666 pandemic resembles exactly what is happening right now with the 2020-2021 pandemic. Coincidence or a calculated murder plan?

47. England as an example.

48. Great Plague of London

49. From Wikipedia, the free encyclopaedia

50. navigation Jump

52. Collecting the dead for burial during the Great Plague

53. The **Great Plague of London**, lasting from 1665 to 1666, was the last major epidemic of the bubonic plague to occur in England. It happened over the centuries-
long Second Pandemic, a period of intermittent bubonic plague epidemics that originated from Central Asia in 1331, the first year of the Black Death. 54. The Great Plague killed an estimated 100,000 people—almost a quarter
of London's population—in 18 months.

55. Wikipedia. 56. I want to highlight the following facts.

57. The origins of the pandemic in 1665-1666 are said to be from Central Asia. 58. The origins of the current pandemic COVID is from China. {Central Asia.} 59. The plague is said to have lasted 18 months in England killing 100 000 people in London alone.

60. Having said that, we argue that the similarities and the circumstances make us believe that they might have recreated the

conditions using digital viruses or engineered biological viruses to recreate the same conditions.

61. The reason why I highlighted the above possible origin of the pandemic is the fact that some world leaders will try to defend themselves against the allegations in this case. 62. Most might argue that they responded the way they did in response to the threat at hand. 63. Acts in the heat of the moment.

64. I think the time frame will rule out most of the above defences. If it was acts done in the first weeks of the pandemic maybe. But a year after no justification must stand. All must be found liable for the above crimes. We recommend the court treat these like any president or prime minister who has carried out crimes against humanity, war crimes, genocide, etc. These crimes are gross, and we must not let any get away with intentional murder. No one must decide who must die and when.

65. Some of them will use the argument of seeing the real threat posed by the pandemic first-hand.

66. As such might argue that they acted in response to the threat at hand. Meaning actions were to save people. They can argue that **THEY WERE INFECTED BY THE VIRUS THEMSELVES AND THEREFORE A VICTIM MEANING THEIR ACTIONS WAS IN RELATION TO THE "INSTANT TRAUMA OF THE NEAR LIKE DEATH EXPERIENCE"** that it is reasonable for any human to use the "force" or method they used as a way to put an end to this.

67. Okay to some extent they might successfully argue that BUT bear in mind your honour that we are dealing with devious, manipulating clever people here. People who will do anything to cover their backs.

68. So, we ask the court to look at those with this first-hand experience OF THE VIRUS and see if they are also the masterminds. We believe they might have deliberately infected themselves after having been given the vaccine before meaning no threat to life. But to fool all of you and trick everyone else. They might have tried to fool the world to take a victim's stance to get your sympathy when they are the ones behind this. To fool the world to be exempted when they are the culprits. Often the first to contract among the leaders might be suspect. We leave this to the court.

69. We also want to alert the court to the fact that you must be wary also of the following facts. 70. Those who become the first ones to methods, techniques, vaccines, etc., or mutations of the viruses, etc. Being the first to discover something might be because of technological advancement, better methods, better expertise, better financial resources, and the commitment of the governments to dealing with the virus.

71. BUT the court must also note that being the first might not necessarily mean or support the arguments regarding resources and technology etc. but also pointing to the source. They might be the originals of the source of the virus that might have been exported abroad and

then waiting for it to roll back to the country of origin before taking active action. Being the first to develop a vaccine. A first to find ways to detect the virus. First to have a new variant of the virus. First to find a cure etc. might point to the culprits. They might have tried to put themselves on the world map on pretences when they are the source to gain possible competitive advantage portraying themselves as the world leaders on false accounts above all through a criminal act. Killing hundreds of thousands.

72. We urge the court to look at all this as a holistic approach. Would it be normal to be the first; 73. To have a leader…mind you where it originated it is associated with homelessness, dirty people who don't wash their hands, body clothes, etc. Mainly people with poor standards and then a leader being the first one might mean a deceptive act on the part of that country. 74. First to have developed the first method to detect this etc.

75. First to have found the vaccine.

76. First to have discovered a new variant.

77. First to have developed a cure.

78. ALL THESE AMONG A SINGLE COUNTRY OUT OF THE POSSIBLE 200 IS SUSPECT. 79. The questions you might want to ask are these.

80. Are they the source? Look at history and documented cases of a similar pandemic. 81. Look at the circumstances. The position they are in would have justified creating a lethal pathogen virus to clean the country and gain a favourable position. A competitive advantage. To herald the announcement of a world leader by holding everyone to ransom. Killing to show power globally and

using the virus to silence other world leaders or opposition. Using the virus to show who is boss even if the virus was natural, they might have created digital or bio-modified to hide behind the original one.

82. I think it is suspect to have everything being first in one country and worse to find a new variant. Mind you we are not talking about a third-world country with poor standards etc. 83. So, we leave the courts to handle this considering the above statements. 84. the court must bring to trial all 200-plus world leaders one by one on an individual basis. It is a crime and as per Tomorrow's World Order, they must all pay if guilty now rather than wait until they are old. We are proactive. We expect the court to act and ACT FAST when the evidence is still there rather than come years later and try to find out what happened. A crime is being committed right now on our watch. The question is what the courts can do. Are they going to change their approach of waiting or might want to modernize even if that means expanding etc.?

85. We have in the past highlighted the issues we have with the court's past dealing with culprits. The law sees no colour or status if a crime has been committed. We speak and stand for everyone and especially the voiceless, yet the most valuable are the women and children often seen as vulnerable and weak. Who ends up like that because the courts and the justice system often favour the elite, wealthy and powerful leaders?

86. Let not any intimidation and sanctions stop you. Only the law shall prevail. Justice shall be the norm under Tomorrow's World Order. A new start. A new beginning. With us, you can count on the law and the courts for peace of mind. We are the leaders of tomorrow. What we want to see tomorrow can only start to take shape if you act now and fast. We leave this in your hands.

87. Note that.

88. There is no personal attack on one nation but when the facts point to a possible culprit, we let you decide. Every one of them who has followed and acted in a manner that resulted, contributed, and aggravated the situation is liable and guilty. Mind you they are all world leaders where there is an express requirement that they exercise sound judgment. Meaning having a duty of care towards their people. People task them to protect their people. When that

fails, we are left with no option but to declare that they are not only
fit for purpose but also criminals.

89. Another factor also is the fact that where there is an opposition
party that did not disobey the government's killings of their
people, they too are accomplices. Accessories to the above crimes
must be charged after dealing with the leaders. No one must be
exempted unless they objected to the demands but were forced not
to fight back. Express support of the government makes them
contributors to crime too.

90. Impacts of lockdown. England as an example.

91. We believe the effects of lockdowns are to weaken the people
even though this is not the intended goal. The number of deaths on
the graph attached from the national statistics office showed a
significant increase double the monthly average to 88 000 plus
during the lockdown in England from 23 March to July due to
Covid.

92. As the lockdown ended the number of deaths declined too but
only to pick up again coinciding with the second lockdown in
England from 5 Nov to 2 December.

93. The truth will only come out after the pandemic, but we can't
wait until then. There is a direct impact of lockdowns on deaths.
The rise in deaths is associated with the lockdowns. A causal-
effect relationship is established.

94. Our recommendations might increase the infection but will
reduce the number of deaths as more and more people develop
immunity naturally the way it is intended without panic and stress
and weakening. People will develop immunity faster than the
approach adopted by the leaders. If they could not produce
vaccines which everyone believed were the cure. They should have
at least encouraged this to happen naturally by providing an
environment just for that. Less stress, more help, and financial
resources and support. It is not about the virus but the system. The
human immune system.

95. We know this might stretch the resources of the courts, but this
is the future the court must modernize too. Greater responsibilities,
and greater expectations on your part too. 96. Being ignorant and
trying to frustrate change just for the sake of it when all that we
stand for as Tomorrow's World Order will benefit the people at
large bringing wealth to all mankind to levels never thought of

before. We stand for the good of all mankind. Resisting on what is good for all mankind is a crime. Harsh punishment because they would rather recreate past evil crimes like the holocaust where people were lockdown forcibly—the idea being to weaken the immune system before diseases ran havoc. THE VERY IDEA BEHIND THE CONCENTRATION CAMPS. IF YOU KNOW THE ORIGINS OF CONCENTRATION CAMPS YOU WOULD NOT BE SURPRISED BY WHAT IS GOING ON.

97. We believe mankind must be guided and directed and if left alone might self-destruct. These world leaders, if the criteria above are fulfilled are guilty and must be punished and removed. We need people who act on behalf of the people. People who would save people and stop investing in wars and military when the people are dying due to lack of enough resources and manmade weakening conditions.

98. The law must be a double-edged sword for those who violate it and a source of peace, comfort, hope, and truth for those who obey it.

99. No immunity to presidents, prime ministers, kings, monarchies, etc. All must be under the law not above the law.

David Gomadza President and Founder Tomorrow's World Order.
tomorrowsworldorder@outlook.com
00447745900178
05 January 2021.

ABOUT THE AUTHOR

David Gomadza

President Tomorrow's World Order
www.twofuture.world

A Stories Prediction

A Stories Prediction

www.ingramcontent.com/pod-product-compliance
Lightning Source LLC
Chambersburg PA
CBHW051359280526
45784CB00007B/3024